Tales of
Teams

Heartwarming Memories of
Hardworking Horses and Mules

*From the Readers of
Farm & Ranch Living Magazine*

Tales of Teams

Heartwarming Memories of
Hardworking Horses and Mules

Publisher: Roy J. Reiman
Editor: Rick Van Etten
Associate Editors: Nick Pabst, Deb Mulvey,
Terry Koper, Henry de Fiebre, Mike Beno
Art Director: Gail Engeldahl
Art Associates: Maribeth Greinke, Julie Wagner
Production Assistants: Judy Pope, Julie Buchsbaum
Photo Coordinator: Trudi Bellin

© 1995 Reiman Publications, L.P.
5400 S. 60th St., Greendale WI 53129

Country Books

International Standard Book Number: 0-89821-150-6
Library of Congress Catalog Card Number: 95-70190
All rights reserved. Printed in U.S.A.
Cover photo by Bonnie Nance.

For additional copies of this book or information on other books,
write: Country Books, P.O. Box 990, Greendale WI 53129.
Code number of this book is 20105.
Credit card orders call toll-free 1-800/558-1013.

Contents

Kindra Clineff

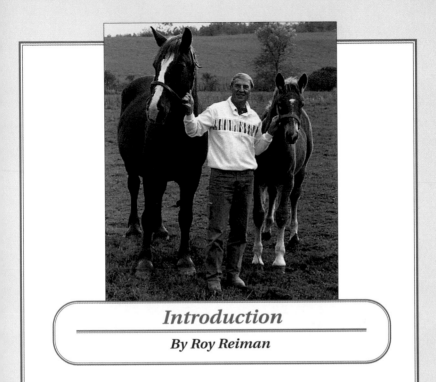

Introduction

By Roy Reiman

I'VE ALWAYS loved horses. Especially draft horses. And that's why I greatly enjoyed helping with the editing of this book. Anyone with a similar affection for these draft animals—the kind that would rather be harnessed and put in a full day's work than loaf around the pasture—is sure to enjoy reading it, too.

While I like all draft horses, I particularly like Belgians, such as the two I'm shown with in the picture above. That's "Maggie" with one of her fillies, "Paige".

Maggie was special in a number of ways. To begin with, I got her as a Christmas gift. This was back in 1981. My wife, Bobbi, had asked me what I wanted for Christmas that year, and I answered flippantly, "I think I'd like a Belgian mare."

The more I thought about it, the more serious I got about my answer. I had always talked about my fondness for draft horses, having grown up driving them on our Iowa farm, but I had never owned one of my own. Owning one now would be something special.

I finally told Bobbi that's really what I wanted, and she went along with it. So I began my search—first for a nearby farm where I could board a Belgian, and then for the horse. I found this mare on a farm near Greencastle, Indiana, and she was a beauty.

She had great Belgian features, a good pedigree, a rich, dark red color (I've always preferred the dark Belgians over the blondes), and she was so gentle we had to throw a bucket up on a tin roof behind her to get her ears up for pictures!

What's more, she was bred and due to foal in about 6 months. That was perfect, because at the time we were launching a new magazine called *Country Kids*, aimed at rural children. This bred mare allowed us to feature and follow her pregnancy for those young readers.

Held a "Name the Foal" Contest

I put aside the mare's registered name and called her "Maggie", short for magazine. Then we urged the *Country Kids* subscribers to come up with a name for the unborn foal. The winner would get a free trip to our farm to meet and pet the little Belgian.

The winning name was sent in by a pair of young brothers from Minnesota. They named her "Paige", a clever and obvious tie-in with "magazine page".

So, there's my horse "tale", but it's not a story about a *team* like those you'll find in this book. You'll find each tale on the pages ahead highly personal and heartwarming, and you'll likely be amazed at the *exact details* these teamsters recall about their horses or mules.

That shouldn't surprise me, for I've often noticed over the years that many farmers can't remember the names of their neighbors...but they *always* remember the names of their last team! The ones featured in this book remember a *whole lot* more.

Gail Denham

Chapter One

Harness Heroics

Harness Heroics

NOT TOO MANY decades ago, horses and mules supplied all of the power needed to work the land. Before the first steel-lugged, single-lung tractors came chugging up the lane, these steady, faithful, four-legged workers could be depended upon to complete any task, in all kinds of weather, year in and year out.

Horses and mules pulled plows, raked hay, threshed grain, skidded logs and moved freight. Like their owners, they enjoyed no "down time" throughout the year, for there was always a job to be done—breaking ground in the spring, cultivating during the growing season, hauling loaded wagons at harvest, or transporting the family through winter snows.

Just getting these jobs done year after year can rightfully be considered heroic. But sometimes these same animals would accomplish feats that were truly "above and beyond the call of duty". Whether performing a lifesaving act or demonstrating remarkable brainpower, the following horses and mules—some functioning as a team and some acting individually—earned not only the appreciation of their owners, but their admiration as well. We're confident they'll earn yours too!

Bonnie Nance

Percherons Pulled Through in Storm

By Weldon C. Swigart, Creston, Iowa

NEW YEAR'S DAY snowstorms still spark memories of Doc's long sleigh ride to deliver our third child…and of our Percheron mares, "Bird" and "Bell", who crashed through miles of deep drifts to get Doc to our home. Thanks to that dependable team, we arrived at the house just in time for Doc to deliver the baby.

The drama began when we woke to a terrible blizzard storming across Iowa on New Year's Day of 1942. My wife was due to have our baby at any time.

Deep drifts on the 7-mile stretch to Creston had closed the road to vehicles. I hitched Bird and Bell to a bobsled and headed out after the doctor. Because of the snow, it took me 4 hours to get to town.

Doc hurried into his hunting boots and storm clothes. We covered ourselves with an old rug to ward off the cold on the return trip.

I'd gotten Bird and Bell as foals in 1936, the year my wife and

HEROIC TEAM. "Bird" and "Bell", owned by Weldon Swigart (center), brought the doctor through a blizzard just in time to deliver Weldon's baby son, Kenneth. Seated on horses were older sons Earl and Marvin.

I were married. I'd begun training them as 3-year-olds, and that stormy night I knew all the time I'd spent was paying off.

The roads were just as bad on the trip back to the farm. We were white with ice and snow as we stepped off the sled, and the horses were covered with frost as well.

Bird and Bell sure earned their oats that night—we'd made it home just in time to help deliver a baby boy my wife and I named Kenneth. As for Doc, his reward was a warm bed in our house, where he slept through the rest of the storm!

'Nell' Knew 'Tricksey' Was Trapped

By Curtis Bowers, Dundee, Michigan

A MARE MY DAD BOUGHT at an auction in 1945 soon showed she was as smart as she looked. If it hadn't been for "Nell", we probably wouldn't have found "Tricksey", another of our workhorses, in time to save her. Nell's insistence that my brother and I follow her led us to discover Tricksey's predicament.

Tricksey had tumbled down a creek bank and landed on her back. She was wedged against a tree, unable to get up, and her struggles had left her weakened.

We were alerted to Tricksey's plight when Nell kept coming to the barn where my brother Dick and I were working. Nell whinnied and raced repeatedly toward the lane until Dick and I dropped what we were doing and followed her.

We paid attention to

PALS IN HARNESS alerted their owner if another horse was in trouble.

Nell because of what my Dad had seen in her when he bought Nell at the auction. She was about 7 years old, weighed 1,800 pounds and had an intelligent look to her. After Dad brought her home, Nell worked well with the other horses on our farm in Defiance County, Ohio.

Dick and I followed Nell to Tricksey and immediately knew we couldn't free her, so we ran home to tell Dad. He told us to hitch up Nell while he went to look after Tricksey.

When we arrived with Nell, Dad tied a rope around Tricksey and hitched it to Nell's singletree. With Dad's instructions, Nell slowly pulled Tricksey to the top of the bank.

The filly was cold and exhausted from spending the night fighting to get up. Dad rubbed Tricksey thoroughly with a burlap bag to restore her circulation.

After an hour, we were able to help Tricksey stand. As we walked Tricksey home, Dad said he was mighty glad he'd gone to that auction and put in the winning bid on Nell.

'Tupsy' Battled Blizzard

By Virgil Axtman, Pewaukee, Wisconsin

I'LL NEVER FORGET one winter back in the 1930's and the gentle mare that saved my life. I was 7 years old and enjoying a week off school for Christmas vacation. After doing the chores on our North Dakota farm, I was getting antsy sitting around the house. An idea came to mind.

"Pa, it's real nice out and the sun's shining," I said. "Could I take one of the horses to see Uncle Marty and my cousins? Please?"

"No! It's too cold out," my father answered. "Besides, you might get caught in a snow drift."

I nagged him all morning until he finally gave in.

"Have your brother bridle 'Tupsy' for you," he said. "That's the only horse I trust you with."

Tupsy was a huge Belgian mare. Not only was she strong, she was very intelligent. We didn't use saddles on our horses because we were too poor. Even if we'd had the money, I doubt that they made saddles big enough to fit our work horses.

My brother boosted me up on Tupsy. It was like sitting on a divan. I could just barely straddle her wide back with my little legs. My father approached as I was about to leave.

Weather Warning

"If anything happens, let the horse have her head and she'll see that you get back home," he said. "She's a real smart horse—horses are smarter than people think.

"Tupsy has gotten me home in a storm more than once. She'll be good to you, so no matter what happens, stay with the mare."

Tupsy and I headed across the fields through knee-deep snow. I tried to get her to go faster, but she had only one speed—slow! I resigned myself to sitting back and enjoying the ride.

When I reached Uncle Marty's house I sure was glad to see my cousins. Time flew by quickly. We were playing in the snow when my uncle, quite a kidder, stepped out on the front porch

"The storm almost blew me off Tupsy when it hit us..."

and looked at the sky.

"Gonna have a blizzard by nightfall," he said.

I asked if he could tell by looking at the clouds or the color of the sky.

"Nope. I heard it on the battery radio a few minutes ago," he grinned.

He lifted me up onto Tupsy and sent me on my way. "You'd better head home while you can," he said. "You don't want to get caught in a prairie blizzard."

As I rode off I sensed uneasiness in Tupsy. She was trotting now instead of walking. It didn't take a genius to tell Tupsy was nervous about something.

Storm Struck with Fury

I hadn't gone a mile when Tupsy raised her head and snorted. I looked and saw a white wall of snow coming toward us.

14

I was never so scared in my life, and there was little I could do. I pulled my hat down as far as I could, wrapped my scarf around my face and braced myself.

The storm almost blew me off Tupsy when it hit us. I tightened my legs around her, clutched her mane and held on for dear life. In the back of my mind I could hear Pa's voice: "Let her have her head." I draped the reins around Tupsy's neck.

GENTLE GIANTS could find their way home even in a blizzard.

Now it was snowing so hard I could hardly see Tupsy's head. Boy, was I scared! I couldn't see where I was or where I was going. Strong winds blew snow against my face, stinging like needles.

The only thing that kept me from going to pieces was that huge mare under me. I knew Tupsy was strong and if anything could get me home, it was her!

Half crying, I kept talking to Tupsy. Encouraging the mare helped keep me from falling apart.

"Come on, Tupsy, you can do it! Come on, Tupsy. Take us home," I blurted over and over as she struggled through the storm.

My heart sank as Tupsy stopped suddenly and turned her head toward me. "Now we're done for," I thought, wondering why the horse hadn't given out sooner.

But the problem was only that Tupsy needed the snow and ice wiped from her face so she could see. After that, whenever she stopped, I'd wipe her eyes with my scarf.

Where Were We?

After what seemed like hours, Tupsy stopped again. This time she wouldn't budge, no matter how hard I hollered. Then she did a curious thing. Tupsy kept moving forward and backward, as though attempting to dig a hole to lie in.

Then I heard a noise. Tupsy had her great shoulder against the barn door. Slowly, she opened it just enough to squeeze through.

With her last bit of strength Tupsy headed for her stall and fell on her side…and her spirit left her. Tupsy's big heart just wasn't strong enough to keep that old body going after fighting our way back through the blizzard.

For me, everything went blank as I fell asleep. Early next morning I felt something nudge me and woke to see my father. I found myself snuggled up against Tupsy's body. Her fading warmth had kept me from freezing. Even in death, the mare's big body protected me.

I'm much older now and have told this story to my six children. Deep down, I'm sure the Almighty has a special place for faithful animals like Tupsy.

Unlikely Team Saved the Day

By Lillian Fowler, Llano, Texas

*I*N THE SUMMER OF 1945, my husband and I learned that looks don't count when it comes to a team's dependability.

Hudson was raising Angora goats back then on our Texas ranch, and he always kept an eye on the weather. These goats are sheared twice a year and at those times must be protected from the cold and wet. If caught out in bad weather after shearing, they can die from exposure.

Our goats had been sheared about a week earlier and we were keeping them near a barn in case of rain.

On a bright August morning we drove 12 miles to town to shop. We noticed a cloud forming in the northwest, and by the time we'd finished our errands it was raining cats and dogs.

Since no rain had been forecast and because it was clear when we left the ranch, we hadn't bothered to open the barn door so the goats could get in out of the weather.

Raced Against the Storm

Hudson drove our old Ford pickup as fast as he could on the slick country road. The motor drowned out twice in creeks we had to cross.

Once home, we grabbed our raincoats and headed for the pasture. About a half-mile from the house we found our goats huddled against an old stone fence. I doubted they'd even tried to reach the barn because the rain had come up so suddenly.

> ## *"We found our goats huddled against an old stone fence..."*

Most of the goats were shivering on the ground and we started to gather them up. We brought one load of crying animals to the barn and went back after another bunch.

The ground had become so saturated from the storm, however, that the truck bogged down in deep mud. What next?

At the time we were keeping a neighbor's team of pretty bay horses, so Hudson harnessed them to an old wagon and we began hauling goats to the barn again.

After several trips the horses balked at pulling a full load. Nothing could move them and the rain was still coming down in torrents.

Last Hope

Hudson unhitched the horses from the wagon, mounted one of them bareback and led the other to the barn. Meanwhile, I went to find our cranky old mule and our one-eyed work horse, "Ol' Brookin'". They were our only hope now.

The pasture wasn't very big and I knew it like a book. But dense fog had shrouded that familiar field and soon I was lost.

To this day I feel sure the mule heard me walking around in the fog. Whenever somebody tried to catch him, he had the bad habit of standing still so his bell wouldn't jingle and give away his location. Eventually, Hudson returned and found the mule and Ol' Brookin'.

Hudson hitched the ornery mule and the one-eyed horse to our wagon. The two of them worked well together, bringing the rest of the goats to the barn.

Unfortunately, not all of our goats survived, but the mule and Ol' Brookin' did their best to help Hudson, and we saved all the goats we could.

That motley but dependable team lived with us for several more years, earning their keep by continuing to faithfully perform their various tasks.

Team Brought Doctor

By Eleanor C. Ahola, Zephyr Hills, Florida

*E*XTRA OATS and a thankful blessing were the rewards for "Bob" and "Maude", a team of strong horses that helped save our boy back in the winter of 1940.

My husband, our two children and I were living in Cayuga County, New York on a farm owned by my uncles. One cold snowy night in February, our oldest boy, Jack, went into convulsions. We called our family doctor in Moravia, about 5 miles away.

Doc made it by car as far as Fordyce Hill, about a mile from our house. My uncles volunteered their team of Belgians, Bob and Maude, to help.

The men quickly rigged up a platform on a front bob and hitched it to Bob and Maude. Uncle Rich donned a full-length coonskin coat with a thick quilted lining and took off across the fields. He soon brought the good doctor back to help Jack.

Doc filled a small washtub with warm water and another with cool water. He dipped

HORSE-DRAWN BOBSLED similar to this one brought medical help to ailing child.

our boy first in one and then the other. The rest of us could only worry about what would happen to poor Jack.

Finally, the fever broke, and Jack fell soundly asleep. We rested a lot easier, too!

When old Doc was sure Jack could get along without his care, he was ready to head back to his car. Doc donned an extra coonskin coat, and he and Uncle Rich rode off with Bob and Maude pulling into the cold night.

After a long time, Bob and Maude trotted back into the driveway, heading for the barn at a fast clip. We were so thankful we gave them an extra helping of oats for their work.

That beautiful team of Belgians has been gone for years. Still, I often recall the joyous outcome of that frightening winter night and ask a blessing for Bob and Maude, my favorite heroes in harness.

Devoted Sorrel Saved Her Partner

By Aileen Anderson, Braham, Minnesota

MY HUSBAND, Henry, and I will never forget the day in 1948 we saw a firsthand example of one animal's devotion to another.

"Chubby" and "Queen" were a large, well-matched sorrel team that faithfully performed all our farm tasks, often under the most adverse conditions.

One day Henry was shingling our barn roof when he heard Queen whinny loudly to get his attention. Henry looked down to see that Queen had returned from the pasture alone. Where was Chub?

Queen seemed worried, so Henry went to the pasture to look for Chub, but to no avail.

Call for Help?

Henry searched a field of tall corn but still couldn't find Chub. While walking along the shore of a lake at the west end of our farm, Henry heard a faint whinny and looked in that direction.

Henry's heart sank as he saw Chub looking at him for help. Only the horse's head and neck were still sticking up from a dangerous patch of quicksand!

The race to save Chub began. Henry hurried back to the barn for a rope. He ran across the road to get our neighbor, Ted, and his team to pull Chub free.

Very carefully, Henry made his way out to Chub and managed to get the rope around Chub's chest. Then Henry pulled

"Henry ran for Ted and his team..."

himself back to safety along the rope, and Ted urged his team to give it all they had. Chub was stuck so soundly in the quicksand that the rope broke!

Henry ran back home for another rope. Meanwhile, I got on the party line and called another neighbor for help. Several others must have been "rubbering in" on the conversation, because they rushed to help rescue Chub.

Another rope was put around Chub, and once again, Ted's team gave it their all. They were unable to pull the frightened horse free.

Henry had to race home again. This time he returned with the tractor. Finally they dislodged Chub, shivering and covered with quicksand.

Chub was led home and tied to the windmill, where he stood in the sun a long time, content to get warm and dry.

Chub recovered and we all relaxed over coffee, rehashing the rescue. Henry and I were sure thankful to our neighbors for the outcome—and to Queen for her warning whinny!

Horses' Calm Prevented Mishap

By Gloria Hartwick, Cass City, Michigan

D RIVING TEAMS of horses during the early 1930's was a lot more exciting for this country girl than doing housework.

It was especially exciting the time I accidentally drove over a swarm of bees…it's a good thing my father kept calm horses!

I was about 7 years old and had just started driving teams on our 80-acre farm in Michigan. We raised cattle, hay, corn, oats, wheat and navy beans. Dad was an excellent horseman and always had big draft animals, usually Clydesdales or Belgians.

One day I was driving the team hitched to a wagon and our hay loader. It was warm and sunny, and by afternoon the job had become tedious. I almost dozed off there on the wagon seat, remaining just alert enough to turn at the ends of the rows without missing any hay.

We were progressing slowly down a windrow with about half a load of hay when Dad suddenly yelled for us to stop and unhitch the horses.

Bees Caused a Buzz

As Dad started to unhitch the team I saw the reason for his concern. Because of my drowsiness, I had allowed the horses to straddle a windrow where honey bees had swarmed! The swarm was a dark clump directly between where the horses had stopped.

Fortunately, the team didn't panic—it was as if they knew their best hope of not getting stung was to remain calm. Dad unhitched the horses in record time, and amazingly, although the bees were buzzing ominously, they didn't make any attempt to sting us.

Dad was very concerned about the horses, but when we were all in the clear he didn't lecture me…he only asked why I hadn't noticed the swarm of bees buzzing over the windrow.

That's all that was necessary for him to say. I was feeling badly enough about causing a delay when we should've been making hay on a sunny afternoon.

That was the end of haying for the day. Because of the bees, the wagon and loader had to be left in the field.

When we returned the next afternoon the bees were gone. We resumed haying as usual, with one exception—this time the driver stayed alert!

Trust Kept Horses from Fiery Fate

By Opal D. Jones, Mayfield, Kansas

*B*LAZING FIRE from a stubble field might have killed our horses had they not been so faithful and obedient to my father.

Back in 1934, my parents, Lawrence and Gladys Clark, harvested their first wheat crop on our farm in Kansas.

An abundance of wheat straw was tall and thick that year. Dad had to burn some of the stubble just to work the field with a two-bottom riding plow pulled by our team of four horses.

The team included three seasoned veterans: "Topsy", a big sorrel mare, "Pet", a tan mare with black mane and tail,

"Mother saw blazing fire surround Dad's horses..."

and "Old Charlie", a tall, gangly, white horse.

On the day of the fire the team also included "Cad", one of two 3-year-olds Dad was training.

Whirlwind Sparked Fire

The team was hitched and waiting a safe distance from where Dad was burning stubble. All went well until a small whirlwind picked up a spark and blew it to where it started another fire.

Mother had been looking out the kitchen window and saw the whirlwind pick up the spark. Seconds later she saw that a blazing fire had almost instantly surrounded the team!

Dad was outside the ring of fire. He had to dash through the flames to rescue his team.

Mother endured a few agonizing moments until the horses broke through the blaze. What a relief it was for her to finally see Dad racing through the flames behind the horses, reins in hand, driving his team to safety.

At the barn, Dad insisted on unhitching the team and removing their harnesses before allowing Mother to drive him to the nearest fire station to have his burns treated.

Firemen took care of Dad's injuries, and then they showed him how to doctor his horses.

Dad Cared for Team

The team was burned most on the undersides of their bodies and on their ears, mouths and tails. They were able to drink but could not eat. Dad prepared a gruel from grain and spoon-fed the team.

To complicate matters, Topsy and Pet were nursing colts. While the mares were being treated, the colts had to be bottle-fed.

Cad, the inexperienced starter, was the only horse who didn't survive the fire. Old Charlie sustained the worst burns, but he lived to work again. The belly hair on this white horse now grew in black and coarse.

Pet lived only a few more years. Topsy lived for many years and eventually came to look like she did before the fire.

They had never been a beautiful, matched team, and they finished their working days as a motley-looking crew. But these faithful three survived the fire and became a team again because they trusted and obeyed the man who loved them.

Dad Wouldn't Give Up on 'Old Lightning'

By Jack Morton, Broken Arrow, Oklahoma

MY FATHER'S kindness saved our family's favorite horse after he suffered an injury that might have ended his life. To us kids, Father's unwavering attention to "Old Lightning" remained an example of how patience ultimately pays

Les Van/Unicorn Stock Photos

BELOVED HORSES were nursed back to health after suffering injuries.

23

off...and of a special kind of heroism.

One day I was unhitching "Old Blue" and Old Lightning after mowing a cane patch on our Oklahoma farm. Just then, my sisters walked up the lane singing *Deep in the Heart of Texas.*

"The stars at night, are big and bright," they sang, then sharply clapped their hands. The noise startled the horses, and Lightning and Blue bolted. I had my first runaways on my hands!

The powerful horses crashed through a fence and charged across a pasture, dragging the mowing machine. They stopped not far away and I raced toward them. I knew something was terribly wrong when I saw Lightning limping.

His right hind leg was cut deeply just above his hoof. I calmed the team enough so we could head home.

Long Walk to Barn

Old Lightning hobbled along bravely. His injury made the short distance seem a lot longer. In those days we had no cars or telephones and our veterinarian was over 20 miles away. My father faced the job of doctoring Old Lightning himself.

Even with Father's kind treatment, Old Lightning still suffered. Despite the challenges of infection and other terrible complications, Father wouldn't give up.

Neighboring farmers visited to offer consolation. Eventually, they'd shake their heads and advise Father to put Old Lightning down. Not Old Lightning! He was the family's favorite horse.

Father made a sling to ease the weight on Lightning's leg. Despite all the attention, it looked like we would lose our beloved animal.

Finally, fortune seemed to smile upon us, as Old Lightning began to show improvement. It was a joyous day for our whole family.

Old Lightning responded well to father's tireless care and to the attentive love from our family. Though he carried an unsightly scar on his leg for the rest of his life, he eventually recovered completely and resumed all of his old duties. My father's heroic determination had won out long after many others would have given up the struggle.

Lightning never seemed to tire of pulling our farm equipment along endless rows of corn, cotton and peanuts...and he enjoyed many more years as our family's favorite farm animal.

Gentle Giant's Gallantry Saved Partner

By Wayne E. Shaffer, Sitka, Alaska

*H*OOVES THUNDERING ACROSS an old wooden bridge echo through my memories of our gentle giant's gallant hour.

If it hadn't been for "Dick", we'd have lost "Queen" in the quicksand.

One rainy afternoon Dad heard a horse's hooves pounding across the wooden bridge over a creek near the house. From the porch Dad could see something was wrong just by Dick's gait.

The 1,800-pound work horse had a reputation as the "Gentle Giant" on our farm in Champaign County, Illinois. Dick rarely moved at a gallop or let anything excite him.

Dick saw Dad, turned and ran back toward the bridge. When Dad didn't follow, Dick turned toward him, sounding an urgent whinny.

Dad climbed the fence. Dick stood still while Dad jumped up on his broad back.

Dick's hooves pounded out an urgent beat as he ran back across the bridge. Dick galloped across a pasture to a hedgerow at the farm's north boundary. Dad saw the source of Dick's alarm.

Frightened Queen Sinking in Sand

Dick's faithful partner, Queen, was on her side, sinking in quicksand. The frightened mare's struggles were causing her to sink faster.

Dad was able to calm Queen, slowing her descent. There was no time to retrieve the ropes and hitch needed for a prop-

QUICKSAND RESCUE. Quick thinking by George Shaffer (at right) and lots of pulling by "Dick" (shown here giving a ride to Wayne Shaffer) saved Dick's teammate from perishing in quicksand.

er extraction. Queen would be lost by the time he returned.

Suddenly Dad realized the answer was waving right before him. Dad saw the big gelding's tail twitching as Dick watched, waiting for Dad to save his partner.

Dad backed Dick up to the edge of the quicksand. He plunged his arms into the soupy sand and fished out Queen's tail. Luckily, the hair on her tail and on Dick's was long enough

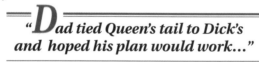

"Dad tied Queen's tail to Dick's and hoped his plan would work..."

to enable him to tie the two tails together with a good solid knot. He hoped his plan would work.

There was no hitch or set of lines for Dad to direct Dick's effort. Dad had to talk Dick through the job of pulling very slowly to free Queen from the quicksand.

The commotion attracted the attention of our other horses. They circled the bank and watched the rescue.

By pulling slowly and steadily, Dick was able to free Queen. The presence of the other horses seemed to calm her as Dad untied her tail from Dick's.

Dad helped the trembling Queen struggle to her feet. For a long while she stood head-to-head with Dick as though seeking comfort from him.

Dependable Workers

For years after, Dick and Queen were faithful servants, pulling plows and wagons and carrying us to school. Dick was so smart and dependable, Dad trusted the horse as our school transportation. Dad would saddle Dick and boost my brother, Paul, and me up on his back. Dick would walk us to school and return home.

Late each afternoon Dad would saddle Dick again and send him more than a mile back to school to get us. On days when Dick was working in the field, Dad would bring a spare horse.

That horse would work for Dick while he picked us up from school and brought us back to where Dad was working. Dad kept our bib overalls hanging on the harvest wagon seat and we'd go to work with him as soon as Dick delivered us.

Team 'Told' of Father's Accident

By Frances Spence, Bushwood, Maryland

TODAY, icy roads pose a hazard for motorists. Years ago, slick conditions made it just as tough for horse-and-wagon travelers.

But there was an advantage with horses: No matter how hard you try, you can't train a car to go for help the way horses could back in the good old days.

One winter, Father was driving a four-horse team to haul a load of fertilizer. He was getting on the wagon when he slipped and fell on the icy road. The wagon moved just as Father went down, and a wheel rolled over his right leg, breaking it.

Despite his pain, he managed to crawl forward to unhook the lead horses, then sent them trotting home for help.

It was already after dark and Mother was getting worried. When she saw the two horses come up to the house, she sent two of my uncles, just small boys then, back up the road to look for Father.

After the boys found Father, they returned home and put a bed of soft straw in another wagon. One boy went with Mother to bring Father home. Meanwhile, the other boy rode to get the doctor.

It's hard telling how long Father would have lain there injured on that icy road if the horses hadn't returned home on their own!

Horses Led Boys to Safety

By Donna Cox, Bellvue, Colorado

WHEN I WAS A CHILD, I could sit for hours listening to my stepfather's stories. One of my favorites was the tale about the horses that saved his life.

It happened back in 1874, when Dad Collamer was 12. He and his brother, Art, would go up into the Rocky Mountains with a team of horses to cut trees and hew logs for their father to sell in his wood yard.

One fall while the boys were high in the mountains, an unexpected blizzard caught them off guard. The wind came up hard and the temperature dropped to well below zero.

The boys huddled together half frozen, trying to keep warm. All they could do was let the team of two horses have their heads and hope the horses could lead them through the blinding storm.

Within a short time the boys were warming up in front of a fireplace, soaking their feet in a tub of tepid water. Their horses were eating hay, safe and warm in the rancher's barn.

The horses had brought them to a ranch house that neither of the boys knew existed. "Those horses saved our lives that day!" Dad Collamer would always declare gratefully.

With a twinkle of pride gleaming in his sky-blue eyes, Dad Collamer added that no machine ever invented will take the place of a loyal team of horses.

Percherons Rescued Family from Fire

By Clint Tenniswood, Melvin, Michigan

*M*EN AND HORSES played heroic roles during the settlement of my home state of Michigan. My father and grandfather often told of how forest fires raged across Sanilac County back in 1881, setting the stage for acts of bravery. One of the bravest men must have been Mr. Eastman. He and his team of faithful Percherons once saved a family when their home was surrounded by flames.

Mr. Eastman had a large farm that had been cleared of timber and slash. That kept his home from being threatened by the great fires blazing across cut-over land.

One day a man rode on horseback to Mr. Eastman's place, shouting for help. A farm nearby was surrounded by fire, he said. Every path to escape was blocked by a wall of flames which was quickly closing in on the family.

Mr. Eastman hurried to hitch a pair of Percherons to a light wagon. They raced for the farm at a full gallop.

Mr. Eastman's Percherons loved to run, and he shouted to the big black horses as they tore right through the fire.

Even as fast as they went, fire singed the horses' manes and fetlocks. It even burned Mr. Eastman's beard!

The family heard the thundering team and Mr. Eastman's excited shouts. They scrambled onto the wagon and the team went flying right back through the fire to safety.

It's tough enough to picture horses running through a wall of fire for their driver. But for horses to risk being burned a second time is a real act of heroism and shows their complete confidence in the driver.

COURAGEOUS HORSES *saved many lives during settlement of state of Michigan.*

Julie Habel

Chapter Two

Phenomenal Feats

NOWADAYS, when it seems like more and more folks have trouble believing anything they don't see with their own eyes, a lot of us still enjoy stories dealing with the out-of-the-ordinary. Maybe that's because there's still a streak of the kid in us, and we're hanging onto a sense of wonder from our childhood. Simply stated, we *want* to believe that extraordinary events can indeed happen.

When the subject is horses and mules, some of these stories have to do with moving exceptionally heavy loads. Others describe triumphing over adversity, demonstrating superior intelligence or accomplishing an unusual feat that defies explanation. And sometimes, the people involved with these magnificent animals were moved—perhaps *inspired* is more accurate—to extraordinary performance themselves.

Winston Fraser/Hillstrom Stock Photo

Amazing Teams Even Worked Blind

By Glenn Quade, Janesville, Wisconsin

OUR WORK HORSES were big and strong and always got the best of care. But in the mid-1930's, veterinarians didn't have the medicine or know-how to treat pinkeye, which was highly contagious. All four of our horses caught it, and all four went blind.

This was right after the Depression, and my parents didn't have the money to replace the horses or the several years required to train colts. The blind horses were the only "power" we had to work the farm, so my folks decided to keep them.

We knew the horses would have to be handled with great care, and they were. We learned, and the horses learned. They did all the farm work just as before.

When we came to a fence or ditch, we had to drive them very carefully. When the horses were on their own, eating grass, they used their sense of smell to find their way around.

They could locate the water tank and the fence by smell. When they got about 2 feet from the fence, they'd turn or stop.

Although I didn't realize it at the time, those big horses taught me quite a bit about dealing with life's adversities.

THAT BEETS ALL! Leslie Meierding of Missoula, Montana hauled this 16,000-lb. load of beets with his six-horse hitch in the 1930's. "My lead team was in great demand to move the 50-ton gondola cars after they were filled," he recalls. "The team had to hang in there, even though the cars moved very slowly at first. Many larger teams quit pulling if they couldn't get them rolling right away."

'King of Load' Almost Pulled Wagon to Loft

By Ophir Vellenoweth, St. Albans, West Virginia

S UMMER VACATION from school meant farmhand work for me. Time has eased the memories of long hours, sunburn and sweat. All that remains are thoughts of delicious farm meals, the grown-up feeling of doing a man's work, and the beauty of the farms in Marshall County, West Virginia.

Dad had a small electric shop in town, so his farming was limited to evenings and Sundays. We had two hired hands—Walter, who lived with us, and Herb, who rented a small farm of his own a half-mile away.

One work horse, "Charlie", had recently retired to the pasture. That was fine with me. One of my chores had been to ride him to the watering trough, and Charlie wasn't always in the mood to have someone on his back.

His replacement, a young Suffolk named "Dick", got along just fine with his new partner, "Barney". Barney was a quiet, sensible Percheron with a sixth

BRAWNY BEASTS loved heavy loads —but some didn't know when to quit!

sense. If there was a problem with the load, Barney had a way of prancing without pulling. When he started his two-step, we knew there was a problem. Barney always knew what he was "dancing" about.

Dick was entirely different. If a load was tough, he got stubborn. He would make it move, or else. Having Barney alongside in the traces often saved us from tearing up equipment. But Barney wasn't always hitched with Dick to save the day.

One hot summer day in 1940, we were using Barney to bring up the loaded haywagon and Dick was hooked to the singletree to pull hay into the loft. The rope fastened to Dick's singletree went through pulleys to the top of the barn, the back end of the barn, along the track where the hayfork ran and down to the hayfork.

Herb stuck the double hayfork into the load. As Walter started to lead Dick into the barnyard, Herb started yelling. I looked down from the mow, where I was spreading hay. Herb had gotten the double fork hooked onto the hay ladders, and one of the wagon wheels was starting to rise!

I glanced toward Dick, and alarm bells went off in my head. Walter was yelling "whoa" repeatedly and tugging desperately at Dick's bridle. His entreaties had no effect on Dick. No load was going to beat him. Whatever he was hooked onto was going to move, or else.

Now *three* wagon wheels were off the ground, and Barney's harness was starting to rise. Holy mackerel! I was going to have a wagon, hay ladders, a lot of hay, a farmhand and maybe a horse up there with me in short order. There wasn't room up there for all that stuff. I made a mad dash through the haymow for a corner.

Then two fortunate things happened. One, the rope broke. Two, my mad dash took me out of the rope's path as it whistled through the loft.

When it was all over, Dick wore a look of satisfaction and accomplishment. Whatever that big load was, he had mastered it. He was still brawnier than anything hooked to him!

Sweep Rake Nearly Swept Woman Away

By Alda Hildebrand, Stafford, Kansas

WE LIVED on a truck farm and dairy in Kansas, farming with an old Fordson tractor and a mismatched but hard-working team of horses. Dad plowed with the tractor, and I drove the team on the cultivator and harrow.

When I was 8 or 9, Dad had to put large rocks on a board across the harrow to hold it in the ground.

We used the tractor to run the old stationary hay baler, and the horses pulled the sweep rake, which was deep, wide, and flat to the ground. You drove down a windrow and "swept" the hay against a bar about 2-1/2 feet tall near the back of the rake until you had a load. Then you headed for the baler.

One day when I was 12 and driving the team, the sweep rake's teeth got caught in gopher holes. I was riding on the "V" in the back and somehow jumped to the front as the rake flipped end over end. The hay bar just missed me. By God's grace, I was unhurt. Dad was petrified, and the team must have been, too, because they ran off and we had to chase them down.

Horses Worked Way into Boy's Heart

By Carl E. Stoddard, Georgetown, Idaho

*L*OG, PLOW, drill or make hay, there wasn't one task I didn't do with horses during decades of farming in Idaho. I was born and raised on a farm in the state's beautiful southeast corner. I've farmed that country all my life, except when I was away for World War II.

In September 1945, I stepped off the bus that brought me home and almost immediately went back to driving horses in

"Horses handled tasks with skill and pride..."

our grain fields. For the next seven years our neighbors and our horses cut an awful lot of grain together.

Those were great times. Wives would compete to see who could cook the best dinners for the threshing crews.

The work was hard and the days were long, but we enjoyed our lives back then. We got a great deal of satisfaction from working with our horses.

"Coally" was one of the best horses I ever owned. I discovered his talent for training younger horses one day in 1938. I'd hitched Coally with "Kernel" for a photograph my uncle wanted to take.

After dinner the team was still hitched up, so I decided to use them on some hay Dad told me to rake. Kernel was inexperienced, but I didn't feel like catching and harnessing another horse.

When Dad came to check on me he was initially upset that I was using a "green" horse. I told him to watch while I dropped the lines and made a round without touching them—Kernel had "learned the ropes" just from working with Coally. Dad smiled proudly and told me it looked like I'd found a perfect pair to work with.

For the next 3 years I drove Coally and Kernel for every job. They handled each task with skill and pride. Unfortunately, Coally eventually became stiff in the shoulders and had to be traded to another farm where work wasn't so demanding.

I missed Coally, but I still had Kernel. We could hitch Kernel with any other horse and have a good team.

We would hitch colts to Kernel for their initiation to discipline and work. Usually they were dependable by their third time in harness.

I drove every kind of hitch there was for farm use. I still miss working with horses!

THEY DID IT ALL. Carl Stoddard posed with two of his workhorses, used for everything from logging to making hay. "Coally", at left, was one of the best.

MILK WAGON. Lenthel Stanton drove this unusual three-horse hitch to haul milk for the Borden Company in Harpersville, New York. Son Homer of Tucson, Arizona says the picture was taken in 1910.

Team Hauled Milk Across Fields When Roads Closed

By John Voegeli, Arlington, Wisconsin

I'VE BRAGGED many times about the team I used to haul cans of milk during the blizzard of 1935-36. Heavy snow closed all the roads, except for state highways and a handful of county roads. For 4 weeks, the team pulled a sleigh loaded with full milk cans 4 miles through fields, over uncut fences, to reach Lodi, Wisconsin. This team pulled a home-made four-row corn planter, too.

Faithful Team Came Home for Christmas

By Alice Roberts, Palo Alto, California

*O*UR HORSES, "Prince" and "Nell", were faithful, hard-working and gentle. They were always ready to pull a load of gravel, hay, fruit or fertilizer at our orchard. As a small child, I considered it a special treat to be able to ride to the barn on Prince's big back.

When I was in my teens, the team was sold. Their new pasture was about 10 miles away.

Months later, on Christmas morning, Papa went to the barn to milk—and there were our friends, standing in their old stalls! They had made their way across a foothill, through town, across the railroad tracks and a mile down our road, then pushed through our barnyard gate.

It was such a thrill to see them and made our Christmas so happy. We were sorry to have to say good-bye to them again the next day.

Bell Brought Mule Trotting Home

By Erlene Leach, Kosciusko, Mississippi

*D*INNER BELLS ringing from our neighbors' farms signaled a daily test of willpower between Papa and his mule.

Back in Mississippi in the 1930's, women would begin ringing dinner bells at around 11 o'clock. The bells had different tones so each farmer would know when he was being called to dinner.

Our mule "Sam" knew the tone of each bell as well as any farmer. Several bells sounded before Mother rang ours at about 11:15 each day.

As each bell rang both Dad and Sam would become impatient, but for different reasons.

Papa always wanted to work up another row before coming in. At the sound of each bell Sam became more determined to trot home for his dinnertime rest.

Actually, this worked out pretty well for Papa. Mother wouldn't tolerate Papa being late to the table.

Papa never had to worry about getting her riled. When our bell finally sounded Sam headed home—no matter how much more Papa tried to do before dinner.

Mules Wouldn't Work Overtime

By Harland K. Speer, Brighton, Colorado

CLOCKS COULD BE SET by watching Dad's mules work our fields in Minnesota. After one pass at plowing a cornfield they knew how long each trip would take. At quitting time they'd use those calculations to keep from doing what they believed was extra work.

Once I tried to get them to make a final 15-minute trip to plow the last row around a field. Somehow they knew it was only 10 minutes until 6 o'clock—their usual quitting time.

They were so balky that when we finally finished the job at 6:30 I wondered whether it was worth the extra energy it had cost *me*.

Another evening while heading home I remembered a piece of work left unfinished. I tried to turn the team back but the mules refused to go.

I tied them to a gate, walked back and finished the chore without them.

Mules knew other ways to avoid work. One time, plowing with a five-mule team, I knew most of them were working way too hard.

The center mule on the wheel team wasn't pulling at all. I switched his position with another mule and he was forced to do his share of the work for the rest of the season.

Horse 'Out-Stubborned' Mule

By Edwin Swartz, Colon, Nebraska

OUR RELIABLE OLD HORSE once taught one of our mules the real meaning of the word "stubborn". Each day at 11:15 a.m. and 4:30 p.m. this mule would begin to balk. The closer it got to dinner or quitting time, the slower the mule would work.

Sometimes he would bore into his bit so hard I couldn't

keep him in line. He'd turn toward home, stomping all over the corn we were working in.

I finally had an idea. I brought our savvy old gray horse in from the pasture and hitched him with the mule. As it got toward 11:00, I told the horse to slow up a bit.

Now the mule wasn't so eager to speed up his pace toward home—he'd have to pull the load by himself, and that was too tiring.

The mule also quit crossing over the rows, trying to turn toward home. That old gray horse was so stubborn he wouldn't give up his ground when the mule tried to shoulder him over!

Dad's Team Demonstrated Value of Trust

By Gilbert Gander, Spokane, Washington

*T*HE WORST OF TIMES brought out the best in some men and horses, including my Dad and his team. During the Depression our team of horses, "Goldie" and "Joe", showed a Montana foreman the value of well-trained animals in the hands of a skilled driver.

Goldie and Joe were sister and brother. They were beautiful buckskins and not the mousy gray ones, either.

Goldie and Joe had a golden hue with shiny black manes and tails. They each had a black stripe running down their back.

They weighed 1,600 pounds each. You'd have had a hard time telling them apart, except for the white star on Goldie's face.

Dad raised them from birth. Dad was so skilled and gentle at breaking them, he could get the team to do anything just by talking softly to them.

With a whisper Dad could back the team a hundred yards or more.

Team Tackled Community Chores

The team worked mostly on our place. But this was during the Depression, and we were given community duties as well.

Dad and the team were working off our water tax on a construction job for a public irrigation canal. A foreman

> ## "*The foreman didn't believe horses would work on such a steep bank...*"

feared he'd have to divert most of his men to shoveling excess dirt from a steep ditch bank. Dad volunteered Goldie and Joe, even though the reluctant foreman didn't believe horses would work on such a steep bank.

Goldie walked along the bottom of the bank and Joe walked along the slope. Joe had to lean against Goldie for support but the foreman was impressed with the way they got the job done.

Goldie and Joe trusted Dad, and they knew their kind owner would not to ask them to do the impossible.

Mule Wore One Big Collar

By James Young, Newman, Illinois

Frank Oberle

THE LARGEST MULE I ever knew of was one owned by my father-in-law, William W. Dement. While working around Shawnee, Oklahoma back in 1923-24, he owned a big mule named "Tom".

Tom weighed 1,540 pounds and stood 16 hands high. Tom wore a size 21 collar.

MAMMOTH MULES
like this one required
especially big collars.

GRAVEL HAULERS. Ernest McNally used this team to haul gravel to repair roads, recalls daughter Beulah Sauerland of Oxford, Ohio. "His team wasn't the biggest, but they always pulled better than most of the others," Beulah remembers. "He never used a whip on them. All he had to do was speak to them." She believes this photo was taken around 1938.

THESE VERSATILE HORSES plowed well but were really in a class by themselves at making hay, says Edward Goetz of Riga, Michigan. Plowing in 1940, Ed hitched "Bill" and "Molly" in front and "Fred" and "Topsy" in back. At haying time, however, one team pulled a rake and the oth-

er team pulled the wagon…and they did so without a driver! "I stayed on the wagon to make the load as the hay loader brought it up," Ed explains. "The teams would follow the windrows and turn the corners on their own, which was good because many times I had hay stacked so high I couldn't see the horses over the load."

BEST TEAM on Floyd Kretzinger's farm in Coon Rapids, Iowa in 1926 was this pair of mules. "Art" and "Jen" were hitched to the gravel wagon and covered with fly nets to keep pesky insects from bothering them. Floyd's son Ron, who sent the photo, lives in Dallas, Texas but still farms the old home place.

Horses Always Knew When It Was Time for Lunch

By Alvin Brand, Broken Bow, Nebraska

I CULTIVATED corn with my dad and uncle in 1941 and '42, each of us with a team of horses and one-row cultivator. My team seemed to be able to tell time because every day between 11:30 a.m. and noon they wanted to stop for lunch. Once their minds were made up, I had a terrible time trying to make them go another round.

One day, "Pat" had such a fit that he stood up on his hind legs, breaking the tongue out of the cultivator. I took them back to feed them, and Dad and I tried to make a new tongue. Dad said that from then on, if they decided they wanted lunch, I should just let them have it!

HARD DAY'S WORK left teams ready for their dinner break.

On another occasion, Dad was unloading hay when the mailman came. Dad left to get the mail and took it into the house. When he got back to the barn, his bay team was gone. He climbed up the windmill and saw the horses about a half-mile away in the hayfield. They must have decided that he'd gotten the hay unloaded and it was time to go back for more.

Another horse, "Pete", helped us start Dad's 1930 Whippet during the cold Nebraska winters. Dad would hook Pete onto the car and I'd lead him down the road until the car started. Then I'd unhook Pete and take him back to the barn.

Once Dad needed to go to town while I was at school. He hooked Pete to the car, got in and told Pete to get going. Pete started walking. When the car started, he stopped. Dad unhooked the horse, turned him toward the barn, then went on to town.

When Dad got home, he found Pete waiting in his stall. From then on, the two of them could start the old Whippet by themselves. I'm sure Pete was happy, though, when Dad bought a newer Ford V-8 that would start without his help!

Mules Left Camp to Visit Their Mothers

By Andrew Olson, Dwight, Kansas

THE ROCK ISLAND Railroad was installing new tracks in our community in 1924, using mules on the dirt wagons, slips and graders. Over 100 of the animals were kept in a mule camp about 4 miles from our farm.

One morning, the camp's mule skinner came to our door. One of his teams had gotten out, and he'd tracked them to our farm, just outside our horse pasture.

When Dad went there with the mule skinner, he recognized the mules as a team he'd sold in Kansas City over a year before. And the mules' mothers were just across the fence!

Dad had used the team to fill silos before they were sold, so they knew where their mothers were and had come home to pay them a visit!

EIGHT-MULE HITCH. Andrew Olson's father used this eight-mule hitch to do all his fieldwork in 1927, after his tractor wore out. These mules were hitched to a tendon disk. For spring plowing, they worked in two rows, four abreast. Pictured with the team was hired man Hans Neilson.

Baler Barked a Threat to Spooky Mules

By Paul F. Richmond, Sarasota, Florida

A FAMILIAR MACHINE can make a new noise so startling it will panic a team of horses or mules. I learned this the hard way while working in 1934-35 with a pair of mules named "John" and "Mike". We were baling straw on a farm near Acton, Indiana when the baler suddenly made a strange new coughing noise.

LOVABLE MULES. Working with mules "Mike" (at left) and "John" threw Paul Richmond at first—literally—but he grew to love them.

The team spooked and took off across the 35-acre field and dumped me right to the ground. They were headed for the road.

I'd heard that mules would not run into anything. I cut across a field and blocked their path into the road. John and Mike ran right up to me and stopped.

I learned to love those mules. Their images and characteristics are still etched in my memory.

Pair of Personalities

John was light tan with a dark stripe from ear to tail. His legs were striped like a zebra, although the markings weren't quite as distinct.

John was curious and would watch every move I made, even when I was behind him. John was cautious and thoughtful.

Mike was red and playful. In the morning I could call John to

> *"The team took off across the field and dumped me right to the ground..."*

a piece of equipment and hitch him up, but Mike would wander off several hundred yards. When called, Mike would shake his head and tail a few times before running over to be hitched.

I taught them to turn left on the command "Haw!" and right on "Gee!" While pulling a two-row cultivator through corn or beans they caught on fast. In no time they turned on the right row without any command, making driving them a lot of fun. In 1936 I went to work for the railroad. I returned to the farm often to visit my friends, John and Mike.

All that remains of them these many years later is a picture of John and Mike standing in a field.

I've looked at the picture thousands of times and each time I imagine John and Mike looking up and trotting over to greet me.

Agile Mules Made Job Easy

By Elvin Brown, Minneapolis, Minnesota

SOME JOBS just wouldn't have been possible without the help of our sure-footed mules. Back in the 1920's in Minnesota my father and an uncle were trying to level a ditch bank. As usual, they had hitched our two mules, "Ruby" and "Ribbon", between four horses.

The ditch bank was pretty rough footing. It was steep and came to a high peak.

As they started to level the bank their horses balked at working on the steep slope. The horses on the right side of the hitch would not go up the bank at all.

My father and uncle prodded and pulled at the team, but to no avail. Finally, they figured a way to get going.

They positioned the animals in different places on the hitch. This time they put Ruby and Ribbon on the right side.

The eager mules got the team going. Father said Ruby and Ribbon worked that steep bank just like mountain goats scrambling along a rocky ledge.

With Ruby and Ribbon showing the way, the men were able to level 4 miles of ditch bank that day. Father said those mules really proved their worth—and showed those horses a thing or two!

'Bill' and 'Bud' Worked on Their Own

By W. G. McClelland, New Carlisle, Indiana

EIGHBORS WORRIED when we left our wonderful team of bay horses standing without being tied. They'd see old "Bill" and "Bud" standing around hitched to a wagon and comment to my father, "George, those horses are going to run off some day."

"No, they won't," Dad would answer proudly.

Those trusty old horses never did run off. Maybe it was because Dad had raised the 1,600-pound geldings from colts.

Dad had a unique way of easing his work load while demonstrating the team's discipline. Dad taught the team to follow with a wagon as he drove a tractor pulling our combine.

Bill and Bud followed along even though they had no driver. This was back in 1943-45, when our horses were beginning to get help from machinery.

Dad had a John Deere 7-foot combine which he pulled with a John Deere Model A tractor. Bill and Bud pulled an old Weber grain box.

Dad had them follow along on roads and into other fields. To our neighbors' amazement, the team was always right there with the grain box when Dad was ready to empty a hopper.

Kent & Donna Dannen/Hillestrom Stock Photo

I drove the team for threshing, filling solos, planting and drilling. It was always a pleasure because Dad had trained them so well.

FIT TO BE (UN)TIED. Some teams were so well-trained they would stand, untied, without even thinking of running off.

Friends Even After Long Move

By Chester Runck, Twin Valley, Minnesota

*T*HE TROUBLE "Diamond" went through to return home earned him a special place in our family book of memories. To this day, seeing the last picture of Diamond standing in our pasture reminds me of his effort to be with us again.

Diamond was a spotted horse we bought as a 3-year-old. We used Diamond on all our machinery, from plows to the bundle wagon, and saddled him to work cattle.

Diamond was loyal, as we sure learned when we had to sell him. Diamond was 9 when Dad decided we could no longer keep him.

We trucked our horse about 15 miles away to a dealer. He hauled Diamond off to Mayville, North Dakota and then to several horse sales trying to get big money for him.

One December morning 2 years later we looked out in the pasture. There was Diamond!

I often wonder, just how long does a horse remember those who cared for him? We had to sell him again, but I know I'll never forget Diamond.

Team Wasn't Snowed

By Vernon Hixson, Clearwater, Nebraska

*B*ACK IN the winter of 1930, some neighbors stopped at our place for dinner. Before long it had snowed so much that they decided to stay the night. The next morning, we scooped snow out of the lane so they could get their car back on the road.

A little later when Dad went out to feed, he noticed that the neighbors had gotten their car stuck about a quarter of a mile up the road. He hitched his two favorite mules, "Ned" and "Barney", to a wagon and put a logging chain in the back.

Without a driver, Ned and Barney pulled the wagon up

the road to the neighbor's car. The neighbor hooked up the chain, and the mules pulled the car out of the drift and the rest of the way home.

Once there, the neighbor's wife snapped a photo of Ned and Barney, then sent the mules home.

Some people might not believe this story, but the lady who took the photo had two children, and they both can vouch for it.

I'm 80 years old, and I keep that photo in my scrapbook to remind me of just how smart old Ned and Barney really were!

Tearful Lesson Taught Boy Compassion

By Gladys DeLong, Fletcher, North Carolina

OUR HORSE "OLD NED" taught my brother a tearful lesson about man forcing his will on animals. My brother, Jim, was angry because he'd just been leaving to play baseball when Dad told him to take Ned and pull out a log that was damming our creek.

When the log wouldn't budge, Jim's anger exploded. He found a stick and began beating Ned.

Ned's head drooped. When Jim went to jerk on Ned's bridle he saw large tears running down our horse's face!

Jim was so overcome that he threw the stick into the creek and wrapped his arms around Ned's neck. He started sobbing and pleaded for Ned to forgive him.

For a minute Jim and Ned cried together. Jim swore to the horse he'd never strike him again as long as he lived.

Then Jim asked Ned to try again. He promised that if the log didn't budge they would head for home.

As they pulled together this time, Ned skidded the log out of the creek and up the bank so fast that Jim had a hard time keeping up with the horse.

To this day Jim says he's never forgotten how Ned taught him that goodwill always accomplishes more than anger.

Accomplished Horseman Got The Best Out of Bay Team

By Clemens Brontreger, Harmony, Minnesota

MY GRANDFATHER was raised in the early 1900's on a Kansas farm where lots of prairie hay was put up on stacks. They used sweeps or buck rakes with one horse on each side, about 10 feet apart.

His father was a good horseman and could do almost anything with his bay team, "Sis" and "Flory". Great-Granddad would ride one and talk to the other. He didn't use lines, just said "gee" and "haw" to guide them.

One day, Great-Granddad's brothers complained that he had the easy job, working with that team. He replied, "OK, somebody else take them." Everyone soon realized that Sis and Flory didn't behave for anyone the way they did for their owner.

Flory's colts and several generations of *their* colts remained part of our family of horses for at least 70 years.

Mules Outsmarted Summer Swelter

By Lee A. Gramm, Peoria, Illinois

DRIVING MULES in hot weather taught me to admire the way these smart animals could take care of themselves.

As a farm boy in Illinois nearly 60 years ago, I could see that my grandfather's mules were slow but steady workers. They seemed smart enough not to hurt themselves by eating when they were too hot.

Once when I was about 10, Grandfather and I were cutting oats. Grandpa put me on the seat to drive the mules, knowing they would not run off with me.

They plodded along in the morning heat, stopping when

they wanted. All I did as they moved was keep them in line.

At dinner, after we took the mules to a water tank, Grandpa told me to put the mules in the barn for a rest.

The mules would not eat for quite some time. After they ate, we watered them again before heading back out to the field.

The mules worked the rest of that hot afternoon at their same slow and steady pace to keep from harming themselves. My admiration for mules has continued to this day.

Capture of Runaways Was Boy's Rite of Passage

By Jack Graff, Colorado Springs, Colorado

*O*UR HORSES "Prince" and "Bill" looked like Mutt and Jeff when hitched together, and they spelled trouble for anyone who tried to drive them.

Prince, who was part Belgian, frequently engaged my father in a test of wills. Bill, who was much taller, avoided confrontations with Father. He reserved his rebellion for people who were more easily intimidated—like me.

One April morning as I was leaving for school, I noticed Prince and Bill hitched to a wagon. Father was a short distance away, looking over a spot for a vegetable garden. The reins were slack, and the team was nervous. Father yelled "whoa" at them, but that only added to their tension.

This was serious. One more shout would jolt them into a stampede. Just as that thought crossed my mind, another loud "whoa" rang out, and the horses' leg muscles flexed. I leaped for the wagon just as the team bolted.

I managed to grab the top of the wagon's end gate and struggled to scramble into the bed. The wagon fishtailed as I held onto the sides, making my way to the front. I grabbed the reins just as we neared the steep descent to a ravine behind the barn.

I gave the reins a pull and was flooded with relief when the horses responded. I steered them away from the ravine and toward a freshly plowed field, the wagon still careening wildly. The thunder of horses' hooves and the rumbling of the wagon seemed to echo in the silence that followed.

Ecstatic with relief, I shouted "yee-ha", encouraging the horses to run to their hearts' content. I was only 12, and this was the first time I'd ever triumphed over this difficult team.

As I guided the horses around the field, I thought about the tongue-lashing I was sure to get. But it didn't matter. I felt changed, 10 feet tall, unafraid of anything.

When I returned the panting, sweating horses to the farmyard, Father didn't look angry, just concerned and a little bewildered. All he said was that I should make sure the reins were snug. To this day, his acknowledgment of my mastery of the team remains one of the proudest moments of my life.

TWIN COLTS came as a surprise to Norvin Rolander's family. When Norvin's dad bought a mare at a farm sale in 1925, he knew she was with foal, but no one expected twins—a rare occurrence in horses. Norvin, of McPherson, Kansas, was pictured at right, along with sister LoElla and brother Irving. The colts, "Fanny" and "Nanny", later worked as a team.

Chapter Three

Memories Lasting & Dear

Michael Schimpf

Memories Lasting & Dear

WORKING year after year with large, powerful animals was bound to make an impression on anyone. In many cases, a genuine relationship based on mutual affection and trust developed between a team and its owners. Not only were they partners, but friends as well.

Handling a team was often the first adult responsibility entrusted to a farm child, and that child struggled mightily to "make good". Years later, memories of driving the team to help Dad make hay or cultivate corn still generate feelings of warmth, pride and accomplishment.

Sometimes, too, there were valuable object lessons to be learned, as was the case in several of the following recollections. There's little question that all of these horses and mules made lasting impressions that continue to this day.

She Still Harvests Memories

By Mildred Kolm, Schuyler, Nebraska

*E*NDLESS ROWS of corn line my memories of working with horses as a teenager on our Nebraska farm in the 1930's.

We were a family of eight girls and one boy. Father needed all the help he could get in the fields, so we girls were introduced to horses at an early age. Father took a picture of me

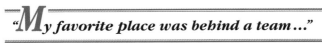

"*M*y favorite place was behind a team..."

standing in front of one of our teams when I was only 2 years old.

My brother was the baby of the family and too young to help when I was getting started in the fields. My older sister

LITTLE HORSEWOMAN. At age 2, Mildred Kolm posed for this photo with one of her father's teams. The family's nine children were all introduced to horses and began helping with fieldwork at an early age.

STATE CORNHUSKING CONTEST was held near Mildred Kolm's home in the 1930's. Local farmers provided wagons, horses and drivers. Mildred's dad was pictured in center foreground.

did the housework so Mother was able to help with the farm chores, too.

My favorite place was behind a team of horses. I helped plow, cultivate, pick corn, make and stack hay.

When plowing, I had a one-row plow pulled by our most gentle team, "Bob" and "Naps". Dad used a two-row plow pulled by four horses.

We cultivated with the same teams, with me working one row and Dad working two. He got a lot more work done than I did.

Work Would Tire a Girl Out

As much as I loved working with our teams in the fields, it was still a tiring job. Sometimes, I was glad to see quitting time come so I could rest.

I'll bet Dad wondered about the value of my help on one job. While running the stacker I was supposed to drop the load where the person on the hay stack wanted it.

Try as I might, I was not very good at this job. I always made more work for the person who had to even everything out after I would drop a load of hay *almost* in the right place.

Some of my warmest memories are of our horses. "Queen" was tall, slender and spirited. When Dad hooked Queen to a wagon, he had to be ready to jump on quick and go. As soon as Dad hooked the last lug, Queen would take off.

Dad usually teamed Queen with her mother, "Lucy". They

always worked well together.

Sometimes Dad would hitch Queen with "Daisy", a fat horse with short legs. They were a comical pair. Daisy had to trot just to keep up with Queen's long stride!

Mules Looked Out for Young Drivers

By Skeeter Pierce, Grenada, Mississippi

A FARMER'S TRUST in his trained mules and horses can sometimes frighten people with little experience in working with large animals.

I remember my aunt's startled reaction upon seeing us kids working with mules while helping my father. It was back in the 1940's when we helped my father build a barn.

Dad was cutting logs. I helped by hauling the logs to a nearby sawmill to be sawed into boards.

Dad always kept good, big mules and this wasn't my first time working with them. I was only 9, but I had already been driving teams quite a while.

As we worked on the barn my Dad's sister drove up in her 1936 Ford. I'll never forget her startled expression when she saw me sitting on a wagon. I was just about to leave for the mill with a load of logs.

"Aren't you afraid that child could get hurt driving those big mules?" she asked my father.

"No," my father answered. "The mules will take care of him." He was right!

Cider Reminds Him of Favorite Mule

By Loyal M. Reinebach, Payson, Illinois

T ASTING CIDER still brings back childhood memories of "Buck", the best mule we ever owned. Once when I was in fifth grade, Buck saved me from the uncomfortable task of having to recite for my folks at our school's "parents' night". We kids had the afternoon off from school, and I was allowed to ride along on the wagon with my older brother, Harold, to haul apples to Boyer's cider mill in Newtown.

Buck was hitched with our other mule, "Jin". We waited in a long line for our turn to come that afternoon. It seemed a lot of other farmers had apples and a taste for cider, too.

It was already dark by the time our cider was ready. Fortunately, the moon was rising over the treetops. It illuminated the 4-mile stretch of rough, rocky, brushy road.

An animal spooked into running would have meant disaster on this rut-filled road. It sure was comforting to be riding behind Buck, who never flared at anything.

When Harold and I got home, Mom and Dad had already left for the school. Mom had left a delicious meal of sweet potatoes and gravy warming on the back of the wood stove for us. By the time we'd finished, Harold said it was too late to go back to the school. Because Buck had held such a slow, steady pace on the way home from the cider mill, I give him the credit for getting me out of reciting!

Young Farmhand Napped on Horse While Cultivating

By Lyle Getschman, Baraboo, Wisconsin

AS THE OLDEST child on our farm, I became my father's "hired man" around age 5. He owned six Percherons, and I learned at a young age how to drive two to four horses abreast.

I also rode a dappled gray mare named "Beauty", pulling a cultivator as Dad steered it through the cross rows. Dad later told me that I often slept on those trips across the field but woke up at the end rows to guide Beauty around.

We planted with a check wire and put the hills on 40-inch centers so a draft horse could pass through. As I got older, I planted corn with a team pulling the check wire at each end of the field.

Trusty Teams Made Her Work Easier

By Viola Petersen, Kensington, Minnesota

M Y LOVE AFFAIR with horses began when I was 4. We lived near Emerson, Nebraska and used Clydesdales to farm. The oldest horses, "Nell" and "Bill", were my special friends and usually received a bit of carrot or apple when I visited them. Over the years, we moved often, and our farm animals became some of my closest friends.

When I was 12, my favorite team was a pair of white mustangs. "Pearl" was flighty and acted superior; "Nancy" was sort of timid and apologetic. But together, the three of us plowed, disked, harrowed, and cut and raked hay. One grain elevator manager said my little mustangs could "outpull" almost every team he'd seen!

GENTLE SPIRIT of workhorses made them good companions for farm children.

When fieldwork called for a third horse, we added "Dick", a bronco. He was special, too, with a sympathetic nature that made him my special confidant. Despite my age, I was doing a man's work, and I missed having human friends. When I was lonely, I'd put my arms around Dick's neck and tell him my troubles. He'd respond with a soft whinny that usually made me cry.

Another favorite team was a blind black gelding named

61

"King" and an arthritic mule named "Kate". When I was ready to start working, I'd just say, "All right, kids, let's go"—and they'd take off.

King's blindness was never a problem. If there was an obstacle in his path, I'd just stop and say, "Up, King, up." He'd raise his foot until I stopped saying "up". I don't remember him ever tripping.

My husband and I farmed with horses, too. Once a severe windstorm broke down and badly tangled our corn. When we took "Bess" and "Bonnie" out to pick it, they used their front feet to push the corn in, trying to find the rows. They did pretty well, too!

Those were wonderful years, and I look back fondly on those four-footed friends who shared so many hours of work with me.

Huge Horses Gentle Enough Even for Youngest Rider

By Dorothy Crow, Macon, Missouri

I WAS 6 when my father brought home a new team of black-and-white work horses. One had a black tail, and the other a white one, so I named them "Salt" and "Pepper".

The horses were so huge that my first question was, "Can you ride those big boys?" My father replied, "Sure can." And we did. Pepper was so gentle he'd let my cocker spaniel and me ride him all day if we wanted, sometimes without a bridle.

Salt and Pepper helped us plant corn, mow hay, plow the garden, cultivate crops and move cattle 4 miles to new pasture twice a year. When we shucked corn, they pulled the iron-wheeled wagon across the long river bottom field.

Salt was the larger horse, and my parents had a strict rule never to bridle him during snowy or icy weather. But when I was about 8, during an ice storm, I did just that.

GOOD LISTENERS. Horses always could be counted on to keep a person's most important secrets in strictest confidence!

As Salt and I were walking down a hill, his huge feet slipped from beneath him. We both fell, and Salt rolled right over me. When he regained his footing, he struggled back up the icy hill to me, nudging my face with his soft nose. Luckily, I only had the wind knocked out of me. I led Salt back to the barn and never told anyone our secret until I was grown.

Spirited Grays Were Dad's Favorite Team

By LeRoy Pauley, St. Cloud, Minnesota

A ROUND 1937, my father and grandfather had mares bred to the same stallion. The offspring were a matched set of dappled grays. They became Dad's favorite team. He still likes to talk about them.

For the first year of the foals' lives, Dad and Grandpa argued jokingly about which of them would give up his foal so the other could have a matched team. Dad eventually got both, a mare named "Lady" and a gelding named "Dick". The two were quite spirited, so they were seldom hitched together.

Grandpa planted all the corn on the farm—at his own pace. According to Dad, Grandpa was perfectly content to sit behind a team of leisurely mules and let the check wire slowly click through the planter guide.

To speed things up, Dad decided Grandpa should use "the gray team". He reasoned that drawing a two-row planter through the heavy clay of Shelby County, Iowa would be just the thing to sap a little of this young team's vinegar.

Grandpa protested vehemently, but finally said OK—provided Dad walked along for a couple of rounds, just to make sure everything went well. Grandpa proceeded to use the team all day.

When Grandpa showed up the next morning, Dad said, "I'll go harness the mules." Grandpa replied, "No, I want to use the gray team." From that day on, Lady and Dick never worked with another horse. With Grandpa at the reins, they planted hundreds of acres of corn.

In 1947, Dad acquired two tractors, and the gray team was retired to the pasture. After 3 months, a prospective buyer asked to see them work together. The only piece of horse equipment we had left was a sickle mower. Dad hitched up the team, and the mower chattered away as the horses went around the yard, proudly displaying an absolutely parallel doubletree.

I still remember those four ears perking over the sides of the livestock truck as it pulled out of the yard. The grays were Dad's best and last team.

He Relished Driving Water Wagon for Threshing Crew

By Charles Hilton, Terre Haute, Indiana

I'VE LOVED HORSES as long as I can remember, but my family lived in the city. Once I built a "horse stall" in my pigeon shed, complete with feed box and halter, just in case a miracle occurred. I gazed longingly at newspaper and magazine stories about ponies being given away as contest prizes.

During my adolescence and early teens, I visited an Indiana farm family for a week or 2 every summer. For a city boy, that was the ultimate—especially the year I was chosen to be the "water boy" during threshing! I drove "Spot", pulling a buggy that held two milk cans of water.

On another visit, I learned how to cultivate corn with a two-horse riding plow. It wasn't too difficult, because "Blackie" and "Joe" knew exactly when to stop or turn around. About all I had to do was guide the plow with my feet to keep from digging out the young stalks. It amazed me that the animals knew to skip two rows of corn on each turn as we moved across the field!

Cultivating Was Pleasant, Peaceful, Barefoot Time

By Joy Schrock, Ontario, California

DURING THE DEPRESSION, three horses provided enough horsepower to run our 80-acre farm near Topeka, Indiana.

We had little money and few clothes, but we worked hard and had plenty to eat from the garden and the truck patch.

When Papa finished working the ground with a sulky plow, I took the horses and harrowed. All day long I'd walk along barefooted behind that harrow, getting the ground ready for planting corn. I loved the blue sky, the fluffy clouds, the killdeer building nests, the meadowlarks singing from fence posts.

At cornhusking time, the horses pulled the wagon through the field. Papa and I tossed yellow ears against the backboard. I worked the outside row so I wouldn't get hit by one of those flying ears.

I remember one fall seeing sun dogs in the sky just as we finished loading corn. On the way to the barn, a cold wind came up.

The next morning, there was white fluffy snow on the ground. "Charley", "George" and "Doc" were in the barn...the corn was in the crib...we were in the kitchen sitting by the cozy wood stove.

What I wouldn't give to follow those horses around the field one more time! I've often wondered how many miles I walked behind them. Now I'm 80 years old and proud of myself when I walk a mile!

HAPPY TIMES. Joy Schrock still fondly recalls "Charley", "Doc" and "George", shown above with her father, and the many pleasant hours she spent following them through the fields.

Grandpa's Belgians Were Like Members of Family

By Kathryn McGaughey, Denver, Colorado

WHEN MY SCOTTISH-born grandfather came to live with us in Nebraska, his matched pair of Belgians came, too. "Joe" and "Jim" had worked on the farm for years, but they were more than workhorses to us. They were members of the family, and we all pampered them. When Joe died, Jim became our most valuable horse, easily harnessed and used for every situation. If a car got stuck in the snow, Jim pulled it out. If a cow got bogged in the muck of the creek, Jim helped pull or lift her. If there was an unexpected storm, Jim brought my sisters and me home from school in the big sled. He often hauled newborn calves from the pasture as the mother cow bawled in protest. We also used Jim to carry barrels filled with corncobs from the pigpen to the house. Fuel was scarce, and the cobs made a quick, hot fire in the Home Comfort range.

On one such trip, Jim got overly anxious to get back to the barn and trotted off at a fast clip, sending corncobs flying in every direction. As strict United Brethren, we *never* swore, but my oldest sister did that day!

Unlikely Pair Always Ready to Go to Work

By Marvin Martens, Shelby, Iowa

MY FAVORITE team of horses wasn't much to look at, but they were still beautiful individuals. "Pete" was a small black gelding, a bronco from north Dakota who was built like a quarter horse. "Lizzie" was born to one of our Percheron mares from a Clydesdale stallion and was marked like a "Clyde".

When Lizzie was 3, my dad broke her one spring morning—and she was working on a disc that afternoon. I was a preschooler then, but when I got older, I drove the team while loading hay. They always seemed to know just what to do. Still, I wondered why this odd pair did most of the work, while our other horses ran in the pasture.

In 1945, when I was 14, I stayed home for 2 weeks to pick corn, which was permitted in those days. Pete, on the left, kept the high-wheeled wagon beside me, and I never had to tell him or Lizzie to move, or even say "whoa". Finally I understood why they did most of the work. At that time, Pete was 27 and Lizzie was 11.

The two were turned out to pasture on Saturday evenings, and they were always waiting at the gate on Monday mornings, ready to go back to work. But horses were on the way out, and we sold them 3 years later. I've often wished I'd had them back in their "retirement years".

Baby, Foal Joined Family on Same Day

By William McGaughey, Denver, Colorado

*I*T WAS MARCH 28, 1913, after a huge snowstorm struck a remote valley in western Colorado. A happy young couple who had homesteaded in the area had just welcomed a new baby boy—me.

Later, when Dad went out to tend the livestock, he found another "baby". A gleaming white foal lay in the cold, bright sunlight. The foal seemed small, even though the mare and stallion were large. My parents named her "Fannie".

Two years later, my parents grew homesick for family and friends in central Nebraska. They loaded what they could into a covered wagon and set out on a warm

MOUNTAIN MEMORIES. William McGaughey's father took a moment to relax in the Colorado mountains where William was born on the same day as cherished family horse, "Fannie". After moving to Nebraska, the McGaugheys returned to Colorado years later; white horse above was Fannie's descendant.

September morning for a 32-day trek over mountains and open plains.

Fannie, her mother, and several other horses were tied to the back of the wagon. Fannie was happy to run along and stay close to her mother. After a few days, the horses learned to follow without being tied.

By the time we reached Nebraska, Fannie had taken her turn pulling the wagon. She was paired with "Peter", who was close to her size at 1,000 lbs.

Once we got settled, Fannie became a buggy horse, pulled the spring wagon and later was used as a riding horse. When I was in first grade, we rode her to school in snow so deep that she had a hard time breaking a trail. My sister's feet dragged across the tops of the drifts.

Fannie's special friend was our pet "Black Dog", who was half collie and half coyote. They always went together to bring in the cows. Fannie lived to the age of 20, and when Black Dog died at the incredible age of 22, we found him in the stall where Fannie had always stood.

Simple Signals Got Mule Right to Work

By Marguerite Hubbard, Hurlock, Maryland

M Y PARENTS' first place was half farmland and half cut-over timberland. During winter, whenever the weather was mild enough, they went out to pull stumps with "Mike", their mule.

Father settled the puller around the stump and Mother held the reins, with Mike geared to the rope. When all was ready, Mother just said, "OK, Mike". He'd wrap the rope around and around the spool, each time stepping over the cable to the puller, until the stump came out.

At hay-making time, Mike was hitched to the hayfork cable to lift bales to the barn loft. On the simple signal, "Go", he'd start pulling and keep at it until the fork reached the loft window. Then he'd turn back to do it all over again!

PLOWING COTTON. Walter Stirl and his father, Carl, used this mule team and two single-row cultivators to plow cotton on their Texas farm in the early 1930's. Also pictured was Walter's brother, Edwin, who was bringing them lunch. Walter lives in Loraine, Texas.

Hardworking Horse Chosen for Cavalry

By Raymond Terpstra, Lynden, Washington

DURING WORLD WAR I, my father took our horses, "Jim" and "Queen", on a trip to Herreid, South Dakota. When he came home with just Queen, we couldn't imagine what had happened.

Dad explained that a man with the cavalry had offered him $150 for Jim. Money was short then, and that was a very good price for a horse, so Dad let him go. Jim and Queen were my favorite horses. Mother said I cried for days.

We never heard anything more about Jim, but I'm sure he did a good job, because he was always a good worker for Dad.

He Watched Grandpa Work From Belgian's Broad Back

By Arnold Humerickhouse, Logansport, Indiana

GRANDDAD FARMED with a pair of handsome sorrel Belgians named "Rock" and "Barney" and let me ride along while he worked in the field. He taught me to mount Rock by walking up the tug strap and holding onto different parts of the harness until I could slide onto his wide back. I still remember how broad he was and how my legs stuck out almost straight sideways.

I always thought the horses were smart because they never stepped on any corn plants while cultivating. I was impressed, too, that when they worked with Granddad's threshing gang, they walked alongside that huge machine without being the least bit nervous.

At the end of the day, Granddad always put me in charge of getting the horses to the barn. I'd climb onto one of the large square posts on either side of the barn gate, whistle a couple of times for the horses and stay there until they walked past, then jump down and swing the gate shut. I was really proud of being entrusted with this important job!

While Mares Plowed, Their Foals Frolicked Alongside

By Arthur Duffield, Hobe Sound, Florida

WHEN DAD needed another team of horses for the farm, he bought a pair of white mares from a dealer. He didn't know until later that both horses had foals on the way. I was so happy thinking of having baby horses to raise and care for.

After about 6 months, both colts were born. I remember watching the mothers plow as their colts ran alongside. The colts would get tired and lie down for a round or two, then they'd be up and off again beside their mothers.

Once the colts were grown, we started breaking them to work, sometimes hitching them alongside their mothers. Just like humans, they learned by example!

Mules Tuned into Hot Weather

By Oscar Prasse, Freeport, Illinois

MY MEMORIES of mules and horses go back to Dad's big teams in the 1920's and 1930's. I enjoyed driving the mules. Dad drove our team of horses.

One sweltering summer we got one hot and humid day after another. We could wear out a team of horses just walking them to the field.

To spell the animals on those hot days I plowed with the mules while Dad rested the horses in the shade. Then he would plow while I rested the mules in the shade.

The mules could stand the heat a lot better than the horses. Even so, at times it got so hot we had to plow at night by moonlight.

Mules Worked Well in Corn

I especially appreciated driving the mules when we worked in our cornfields. Unlike our horses, the mules never stepped on the corn and broke it down when we made our turns at the ends of the fields.

I liked our horses, though they never seemed as smart as our mules. Each morning our mules would find their own way to water. Then they'd walk right to the piece of equipment they'd been hitched to the day before.

We had to lead the horses to water and then to an implement, even if it was one they pulled the day before.

When our mules were too hot they'd go to the water tank and dunk their heads clear up to their eyes. They'd shake their heads all over in the water but would not drink until they were cooled down.

Cool Mules Found Stalls

Then the mules would go to the barn and find their own stalls. They also would not eat until they cooled down, keeping themselves from getting sick.

We would have to lead the horses to water and to the barn. We also had to watch them to make sure the horses didn't hurt themselves by eating or drinking too much after working up a good day's sweat.

When we made hay we drove the mules on a hay rope to pull the tow fork up to the mow. For this chore Dad would just talk to them, directing them where to go.

We worked the mules like this all summer. They were so smart, Dad could just talk to them and we could get the work done without using a driver.

Clever Mules Kept Teen on His Toes

By Lester Askins, Miamisburg, Ohio

O NE DAY when I about 10, my dad was harrowing corn and stopped to talk with a neighbor. I picked up the lines, told the horses to go, and they did. From that day on, Dad trusted me to work the team.

A couple of years later, I started plowing corn and tobacco for my uncle, using his horses. Soon after, he traded the horses for a team of mules, and I enjoyed them from the start.

The mules were steadier, with smaller feet, so they didn't trample so much of the crop when we turned at the end of a row. Mules are smarter than horses, too. A mule won't drink too much water when he's hot, and he won't overeat even when he has the chance.

Later on, when Dad found a factory job, he turned the farming over to me and bought a large pair of white mules, "Jack" and "Jerry". Jack was very nervous; he'd get excited at almost anything. Jerry was always calm—except when he saw a crawdad hole. Every time we plowed along our ditch, I always knew when he saw one, because he walked around it, not over it.

Working with mules was fun, but I had to be alert and out-think them. If they got lazy, I'd stop, cut a switch, and get back on the plow. Then when I told them to move, they really *moved*.

They always let me know when it was time to stop for the day. They'd slow down, look toward the barn, and "hee-

haw", acting too tired to take another step. But as soon as I un-
harnessed and turned them loose in the pasture, they'd turn
around fast, kick, and then run the full length of the field. After a good run, they'd
get down and roll in
the dust.

Working with
mules was a chal-
lenge, but they always
did the best work for
me.

"JACK" AND "JERRY" were a
big help to Lester Askins on his
father's farm. The mules were
challenging at times but always
put in a good day's work.

Recalls Remarkable Horsemen

By Frances Spence, Bushwood, Maryland

A PLEASANT SURPRISE was waiting for Father once years
ago when he returned to the barn after dinner. A newborn colt was standing in the stall with our mare, "Kate".
She'd foaled while still wearing her harness and collar.

Kate had worked the morning behind a harrow with three
other horses. At dinner the men removed Kate's bridle but left
her harness on and put her in a box stall.

After eating they returned and saw the beautiful bay mare
had just given birth to a pretty brown colt. Pop smiled and
patted her.

Off came the harness and collar. Work was over for Kate so
she could care for her colt.

Kate was a good mother and quite a worker, too. We once
met a man who said he'd watched Kate and "Topsey", another of our horses, and Father snake logs out of our woods.

Father just spoke softly to direct their efforts, the man said.
He also told us he'd never before seen a man and his animals

work so well together.

Uncle Willie's Skills

Dad was good, but he said Uncle Willie was even better with horses. How the horses would work for Uncle Willie!

I was with Uncle Willie once when he and his team showed their skill by pulling a wagon out of the mud. It was loaded with fertilizer and the wheels were buried to the hubs.

The stout team pulled toward one side and then toward the

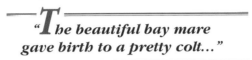

"The beautiful bay mare gave birth to a pretty colt..."

other. Uncle Willie called and whistled to the horses and never used a whip.

The horses worked so hard for him they were almost down on their knees trying to pull the wagon out of those deep, muddy ruts. Finally the wagon rolled out of the mire.

I remember those horses very well. "Fanny" was the lead horse and "Mike" the off-lead. "Old Bell" was under saddle and "Fly" was off-wheel.

Mother smiled when we returned home. I was proud riding with Uncle Willie behind that great team. Father said that Uncle Willie was better at getting horses to pull than any other man he ever knew, and I'd just seen an example firsthand!

Sleigh Bells Added to Yuletide Spirit

By Georgia Krieg, Graceville, Minnesota

DURING WINTER, snow always blocked the road from our farm to the school. One year, as Dad prepared to take us to the school Christmas program, he attached a long leather strap with bells to the horses' harness and hitched the team to a bobsled.

The whole family climbed in for the half-mile ride across the river and the neighbor's field to the school. When we arrived, we found other families standing in the doorway. They'd been listening to the bells ring as the horses ran along.

I also remember working in the field with Dad when I was 17. I had such a toothache that I kept stopping the horses so I could hold onto my cheek. Anytime I spotted Dad coming over a hill, I'd get back to work. The horses got to rest a lot that day!

Another time, Dad stopped the horses and buggy just outside the house and ran in quickly to get something. While he was gone, the horses ran off—but they didn't get far. They ran straight toward a tree, and one horse ran to the left of it and the other to the right!

'Prince' Proved Dad Knew His Horsepower

By Warren L. Peterson, Hutchinson, Kansas

BIDDING AT AUCTIONS could get a farmer in trouble if he didn't keep careful track of what was going on.

Back in the 1930's when I was a teenager on our Kansas farm, an auction got Dad in a little hot water at home. Dad was bidding but not paying close attention as they auctioned off a workhorse.

Just as today, farm auctions back then were also social affairs. Maybe Dad was catching up on gossip when he saw

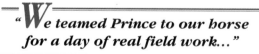

"We teamed Prince to our horse for a day of real field work..."

the finger pointed at him as final bidder on "Prince", a horse he hadn't really intended to buy.

Did Dad ever catch it from Mom when we got home! It got even worse when she found out that horse hadn't been broken.

Well, we still decided to keep Prince. That's when things got pretty exciting for me.

I had to help break him. What an experience that was for

a young fellow who'd never even witnessed a horse being broken.

Dad and I took things slowly. We hitched Prince to an old reliable horse who would hold our untrained animal back.

Getting a harness on a horse as tall as Prince was always an interesting event for a boy. Fortunately, Prince was gentle and generally cooperative.

One time, however, the playful Prince did take advantage of me. As I leaned over to pick up a neck yoke, he bit me on the backside.

Prince Pays Off

Eventually we teamed Prince with our experienced horse and hitched them to a cultivator for a day of real field work. Prince was so strong and had such stamina, we had to hitch a fresh horse to him for the afternoon's work.

At the end of the day Prince was still going strong. He seemed proud and looked as though he was trying to tell us he was worth way more than anyone had wanted to bid at the auction.

Dad Used Team to Take Daughters to School

By Ferne Held, Norfolk, Nebraska

M Y FAVORITE team was the one Dad used to take my sister and me to school in northern Nebraska. During winter, we rode in a buggy with side curtains to keep out the cold and snow.

The horses were a well-matched team of bays named "Queen" and "Browny". Browny was blind in the left eye so he was always hitched on the right side. They were gentle but had lots of spirit and always worked hard mowing, raking and hauling hogs to market.

It was always a pleasure to see them waiting for us with Dad when school let out at 4 o'clock!

Mules Took Theirs out of the Middle

By Darlen Roe, DeSmet, South Dakota

GRANDPA'S STORY of a neighbor's mules shows just how well trained they were. Grandpa often talked of a team of mules a neighbor trained. The mules hauled grain on their own when in the farm country near Hazel, South Dakota.

This came in handy at threshing time. The neighbor didn't need a hired man to drive the mules.

Watching that team work alone was amusing. Well, it was unless you were driving another wagon and saw them clomping right at you, Grandpa said.

The neighbor's mules always ran right down the middle of the road, forcing Grandpa's horses to head for the ditch. Grandpa said that this showed that mules were smarter than horses.

I don't know. Maybe the mules just weren't smart enough to stay on their own side of the road!

Never Forgot Their Trusty Horses

By Violet Laudner, Dumont, Iowa

FOND MEMORIES of our faithful horses were all we had left after the team was replaced by our first tractor. My husband, Russell, and I started farming in Iowa in March of 1940. We started with horses because this was back before anybody in our part of the country had a tractor.

We had one of the nicest teams around. They were "Billy",

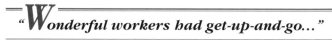

"*Wonderful workers had get-up-and-go...*"

a bay, "Queen", a gray, "Molly", a bay, and "Susie", a sorrel.

We loved our horses so much because they did everything for us, hitched or saddled. They were wonderful workers and had lots of "get-up-and-go". They worked hard and trusted us

FARMING PARTNERS. Changes in farming methods forced a reluctant Russell Laudner to part with the last two members of this team in 1960 when he bought his first tractor.

even when things were dangerous.

One spring, torrential rains flooded the West Fork. Russell rode Susie down to the river rounding up cows and little calves. They were in danger of being stranded by high water or carried off by the swift currents.

Susie Swam River

Russell and Susie eventually tracked down all the cows and calves. They all had to swim the river, Russell riding on Susie, pushing the cows and calves to reach safety on the other side. Susie never hesitated to enter the water, and Russell said later she would do anything for a friend.

We kept Susie and Billy until time caught up with us. In 1960 we finally had to buy our first tractor to keep up with the changes.

It was heartbreaking to sell Susie and Billy. It was such a sad day when we watched them leave our farm in a truck. We loved those horses and never forgot them.

Runaway Teams Made for Tense Moments in Field

By Dorothea Grosse, Lincoln, Nebraska

I'VE LOVED HORSES since the age of 4, when my grandfather first let me drive his team after coming in from the fields.

My first experience with runaways came when I was about 12. I was raking hay as my father and the hired man stacked it. Something spooked my Percheron and Clydesdale team, and they ran into another stack, breaking the wagon tongue and throwing me right under their neck yokes.

When I came to, the horses were prancing up and down, but didn't step on me. I wasn't hurt, except for a few bruises—and my wounded pride.

Another incident occurred when I was a teenager, driving a six-horse hitch to disk. As I was hooking up, the hired man came into the same field to harrow and wanted to make sure it was dry enough.

When I saw him mount a saddle pony, I decided not to hitch up my last two horses. Instead, I walked around the disk to take off the reins so the horses wouldn't bolt. Then the hired man let out a whoop, and the team took off—just as I moved my foot outside the disk!

Dad had some experience with runaways, too, but a mule named "Jack" saved his life many times. If Dad said, "Whoa, Jack", he'd do exactly that, stopping and digging his hoofs in.

Once, on a threshing crew, several teams got spooked and ran, including Dad's. But when he yelled, "Whoa, Jack", that mule left skid marks 15 to 25 feet long!

Dad's Wagon Was a Throne for Colorado Girl

By Donna Cox, Bellvue, Colorado

RIDING ALONG on our wagon with my stepfather, Dad Collamer, I felt like a queen on her royal coach.

What an elegant feeling it was just sitting next to this great man while the wind blew gently through my hair. These are some of my happiest memories of growing up in Colorado. Horses were always important in our family. As a young man Dad Collamer pulled a wagon loaded to the brim with borax with a team of 20 mules.

After a year of driving that rough route, Dad settled down to marry and raise a family. Dad Collamer followed in his father's footsteps and opened a wood yard in Fort Collins.

For years Dad and his horses made the rounds about town,

hauling wood for cook stoves, heaters and fireplaces. Horses also were a remarkable way to advertise his wood yard.

Dogs Barked but Children Loved Horses

Everyone loved watching Dad and his team of two large workhorses go by. Sometimes dogs barked and children laughed with joy as they passed along the streets.

Dad Collamer broke his own horses. They were so well trained all Dad had to do was whistle and cluck to tell them what he wanted.

In the mid-1950's, progress finally caught up with Dad Collamer and his horses. Dad was asked to stop using horses

> "*Horses were a remarkable way to advertise Dad's wood yard...*"

because they were slowing down auto traffic.

Many people were distraught when Dad had to stop using his team. Folks missed the familiar, comforting clip-clop of the horses' hooves as they plodded along the streets. They also missed petting the friendly animals when they were stopped so Dad could unload wood.

The horses Dad used at this time were "Pete" and "Dick". They were retired to a corral in our back yard. Dick, a younger horse, eventually was sold to a ranch.

Pete stayed in the corral and liked giving children bareback rides. Pete enjoyed his easy retirement as the pet of his kind owner—Dad Collamer.

Runaway Team Left Trail Of Broken Equipment

By Don Marshall, Eldorado Springs, Missouri

MOST OF OUR horses were a bit overworked, but one team was always ready to go, stepping high even at the end of a long, hard day. Dad usually worked that team himself, but one day he decided I could use them to cultivate corn. I was so proud!

After finishing with an old walking cultivator, we started back for the house. It was a hot day, and when we came to a small creek, our cows were in the water. For some reason that scared the horses, and they took off.

By the time they got to the barn, a half-mile away, all they had on was their collars. Their path was strewn with harness and cultivator parts.

I was sure Dad would be angry, but he didn't say so much as a rough word to me. It was a long time before I got to work that team again, though.

Quirky Plow Horse Gave New Farmhand a Scare

By Jo Carey, Skwentna, Alaska

WHEN DAD moved us from town to our new farm, two horses were part of the package. "Lady" was a 26-year-old mare who pranced around as if she were a thoroughbred. "Old Dick" was, despite his name, 7 years younger, and knew he was a plow horse.

During the week, Dad worked in town, leaving my mother, sisters and me to tend the farm. We had no trouble mowing, feeding hogs and milking cows, but driving Lady and Old Dick with the ancient cultivator was beyond us. Dad hired a handsome 16-year-old schoolmate of mine to work our cornfields.

On his first day, Bob arrived early to hitch up the team. Dad was at work, Mother was running errands, and I was left to see that Bob got his lunch.

As I was cooking, I heard Bob running toward the house, shouting, "He's dying! Old Dick is dying!" When I asked what had happened, he said Dick had fallen and was shuddering—obviously in his death throes.

Dad had forgotten to give Bob an important piece of information: Old Dick was subject to seizures. He'd fall, shake a bit, then rise to his feet, ready to follow wherever Lady might lead. Sure enough, by the time Bob returned to the field, Dick was ready to finish cultivating and gave him no problems the rest of the day.

'Babe' and Brood Took Top Prize at Ag Fair

By Ethel Tschampel, Merrill, Iowa

I N 1935, my dad took his brood mare, "Babe", to our community's "Ag Days", along with five of her colts. Babe led the parade, with the colts following behind.

The horses won the grand prize of $10. The judge thought this was a sight that might never be duplicated, since tractor power was beginning to replace horses.

Within the following year, one colt was traded in for a new grass mower. Two others were traded for a 10-foot grain binder and wagon box.

But we kept another colt, "Dewey", who matured into a hardworking 2,000-lb. horse. He alone pulled every car out of the farmyard after a downpour drenched my sister's wedding reception in 1944!

PRIZE-WINNING BROOD. Ethel Tschampel's father and sister posed with brood mare "Babe" and her five colts after winning grand prize in the "Ag Days" parade in Merrill, Iowa in September 1935.

'Queen' and 'Maud' Saved the Day

By Wendel Wunschel, Monroe, Wisconsin

*I*T WAS a cold night in late October in the 1930's when our barn burned down. No one ever knew exactly what caused the fire, but the strong west wind didn't help matters any. It fanned the flames so that by the time we awakened, there was barely enough time to free the livestock.

Luckily, we were able to save all of our animals, including our horses, calves, and a big Holstein bull. But winter was right around the corner, and we were now without a barn. And winters in Green County, Wisconsin were usually very long and very cold.

Our neighbors offered to help us put up a new barn, but it had been a rainy fall and most of our roads were quagmires. Getting in the materials for a new barn was going to be very tough.

Two of our workhorses, "Queen" and "Maud", saved the day. They were always determined to prove that they could pull any load they were hitched to, and in spite of the mud, they hauled in all the lumber that was needed for the barn-raising.

Thanks to the gallant effort of those two big-hearted horses, we had our new barn before winter set in.

Rescued Horses Made Unlikely Teams

By Alice Schumacher, Great Falls, Montana

*M*Y FATHER had a dependable team of horses on our Oregon homestead in the early 1900's, but if he saw a poor animal that needed TLC, he couldn't resist rescuing it. That's how we acquired "Ned" and "Daisy".

Ned was a rangy brown horse with a big lump behind one ear. The lump was unsightly, but it didn't interfere with his gentle disposition. Ned devoted himself willingly to whatever task was at hand.

Next came Daisy, a large black horse whose right front foot had suffered a long-ago injury that left it rounded on the bottom. She looked like she was walking over a small bowling ball. Riding her was like being on a ship on the high seas.

One day when Dad had finished plowing, I begged to ride Daisy back to the barn. At 8, I was already an accomplished horsewoman and sat loosely across the work harness, dangling my feet.

Daisy lurched along contentedly until she had to cross a small ditch. The rolling motion dumped me headlong into the dirt. In all my years on the homestead, it was the only time I ever fell off a horse. Even Daisy seemed surprised.

On another occasion, Dad heard about a fine Percheron for sale, cheap. "Eagle" was a huge dappled gray, powerful yet gentle. His teammate had died, and his owner had no suitable horse to work with him. Neither did Dad, but that didn't stop him from buying the big gray.

Eagle dwarfed every other animal we owned. He couldn't

YOUNG HORSEWOMAN Alice Schumacher, shown here aboard "Bluebell", has fond memories of her father's mismatched workhorses.

be used on any of our equipment by himself, and he was too big to use as a saddle horse. Even if another horse of comparable size had been available, Dad couldn't have afforded to buy it.

The only thing Dad could do was hitch Eagle alongside our best puller, "Bob". The result was that when Eagle leaned into the collar, Bob was forced back onto the doubletree. Eagle did all the work; Bob was hauled along for the ride. As teammates, they were a hopeless match...or mismatch, rather.

Eventually Eagle was relegated to the role of farm mascot. My mother, who never tried to ride any of the other horses, took a liking to him. She sat on his wide back sideways, since her legs weren't long enough to straddle his girth, and they happily moseyed along through the sagebrush.

Whatever the Weather Team Was on the Job

By William Parnitzke, Saukville, Wisconsin

WHEN I TOOK over a dairy operation for an injured neighbor at age 16, I worked with a brown bay gelding, "Barney", and a sorrel mare, "Peaches". They were so reliable that they had a better record of being on the job every day than the U.S. Post Office!

And, like postal employees, Barney and Peaches worked in all kinds of weather. They were "sharp-shod", wearing shoes with pegs, and could run on the road in ice, snow or rain. During winter, they pulled large red oak logs from frozen hillsides. They also cut much of the area's canning-pea crop with a swather and a 6-foot mower.

When I started working with the team, my first challenge was harnessing Peaches, who outweighed Barney by 100 lbs. I had to pile the harness in my right arm and then throw it across her with a mighty swing. It was no easy task—Peaches was wide, and I was only 5-foot-7!

Hard Work Was No Sweat For Energetic Geldings

By Lavern Zachrich, Defiance, Ohio

MY FAVORITE working team was a pair of gray geldings named "Fred" and "Prince". My father bought them when they were 4 and 5. The brothers weighed around 1,800 lb. each and wore 24-inch collars.

They were a little skittish around the separator at threshing time but always had plenty of pep. We could plow 2 acres a day with a 12-inch walking plow, and they'd still want to run the 1-1/2 miles home to the barn. No matter how hot it was or how hard they worked, they never panted.

Prince died at 18, and Fred died the following year—of a broken heart, I think.

PEPPY TEAM. Lavern Zachrich (at left) and brother Charles were photographed with energetic geldings "Fred" and "Prince" in 1928. Lavern recalls that even after a full day of plowing, the horses wanted to run all the way back to the barn.

Bug Bite Triggered Runaway

By Neva Gruver, Scott City Kansas

I WAS 11 back in the early summer of 1928, cultivating corn on our Washington County Farm. I was driving "Nick" and "Charlie", a team I'll always remember, although not very fondly!

As we moved along, I used my feet to guide the shovels around the corn. All of a sudden I heard a buzz.

I looked up to see a very large horsefly land on Nick's rump. Before I could do anything, Nick lurched forward.

'Whoa' Wouldn't Stop Them

I yelled "Whoa!" as I jerked on the lines, but it didn't do any good. Charlie just jumped forward to keep up with Nick.

Frightened for my safety, I jumped to the ground. I pulled the swinging seat loose and let the horses and cultivator go.

They ran up a hill and into a big cornfield. There they just kept running as fast as they could, around and around in a big

> "*I* pulled the seat loose and let the horses go..."

circle, still dragging along the cultivator.

I ran about a quarter of a mile home and found Dad in the workshop. Dad sent me to the house to rest while he went after the team.

Dad got to the field and saw that Nick and Charlie were still running full speed, the cultivator clattering along behind. Fortunately, the team was running in the same circle, so not much corn was being destroyed.

Talking Slowed Tired Team

To slow them down, Dad did a lot of talking to the horses as they'd dash by. Finally, they slowed enough so Dad could grab Nick's bridle and get them stopped. Dad led the hot and tired team to the barn.

While waiting in the house I worried that Dad might not let me cultivate again. It was one of my favorite jobs, especially since I usually worked with Dad.

As soon as he saw me, Dad said I had done the right thing by letting the team go when Nick took off. Dad said I could have been hurt if I had attempted to stay on the cultivator and stop the runaway team.

I was able to cultivate again, but never while driving Nick and Charlie!

'Betsy' 'Bused' Kids to Class

By Dr. Arthur W. Allen, Laurel, Montana

WHEN I was a youngster, we lived on a farm in Iowa. Our father, William, had moved our family there from Chicago. The Iowa River ran right alongside our vegetable garden.

School was about a mile from our farm. On rainy days Dad would drive us to school in the Model T. But on sunny days, our transportation was "Old Betsy", one of our workhorses.

Dad bridled up Old Betsy, then invited all three of us, Lillian, Margaret and me, to hop up on her back.

Over the river and through the woods to Glenwood School we would go. We would tie Old Betsy in the school yard during the day while we were inside.

Old Betsy never needed to be guided home. She knew the way and her rides sure made getting to and from school a lot easier!

New Gloves No Help When Horses Bolted

By Oscar Van Lieu, Jonestown, Pennsylvania

IN THE MID-1920's, when I was about 12, I was helping my father get ready to take a load of corn and oats to the mill. I sat on the wagon seat while Dad hitched the horses to the wagon. Just as he snapped the last trace, the horses lunged and galloped off.

It was winter, and I was wearing a brand-new pair of stiff leather mittens, so I couldn't get a good grip on the lines. I yelled "whoa" and tried to pull, but the lines kept slipping through my hands.

The horses galloped into a hayfield behind the barn and ran around in circles. Dad grabbed a pitchfork and tried to head them off, but they paid no attention. They ran through a gate, careened down a steep hill, and stopped when the front right wagon wheel rammed into the engine house.

My father calmly climbed into the wagon, backed the horses up and started for the mill. He made the team trot right along, telling them that if they were so eager to "go", now was the time!

Moody Mules Taught Him
The Meaning of 'Stubborn'

By Henry Kipfer, Hicksville, Ohio

T HE SUMMER I was 13, I went to my uncle's Indiana farm to help out. That was the summer I learned the meaning of the phrase "stubborn as a mule".

My uncle's mules were large, beautiful—and stubborn. In the mornings, we couldn't get them out of the pasture to harness them. The only solution was to chase them around the field with the Oldsmobile once or twice. After that, they were quite willing to go through the gate and into the barn.

The mules made a hobby of running away with anything they were attached to. They always had sharp bits in their mouths, but no matter how much I pulled on the lines, I couldn't slow or stop them.

One day they started to gallop on a rough gravel road, flying around the corners so fast I expected the wagon to roll over any time. Luckily, they stopped just as they got to our barn.

Another time, they took off toward the woods, flattening a

gate along the way. I was so frightened that I leaped out of the wagon as they jolted across a creek. They didn't stop until they reached the woods, where the wagon got caught in the trees.

The last time they ran away, I was in the field with a roller, smoothing freshly worked ground. I was sitting on the front of roller, with scarcely anything to hang onto, when they started running. They very nearly threw me ahead of the roller.

I felt fortunate that I didn't have to stay at the farm long enough to experience a fourth episode.

Riding Horse Filled Void Left When Team Was Sold

By Gloria Coveleski, Groveport, Ohio

WHEN DAD SWITCHED to tractors, he decided to sell our last team of work horses. I was 10 years old and had spent many hours riding "Dick" and "Charlie" as Dad worked them in the field. I told Dad that if they were leaving, I was going with them!

Dad promised to find me a riding horse to take their place. About 2 months later, he bought a 4-year-old horse, bridle and saddle included, for $150. The horse had no name, so I called him "Butch".

Butch was a wonderful pet, ridden not only by me, but my father, my brother, and many of our friends and neighbors. Dad certainly got his money's worth, as Butch was part of the family for 36 years.

Chuck Wyrostok/Appalight/Hillstrom Stock Photo

A.M. Wettach

Chapter Four

Rip-Snorters, Rib-Ticklers & Real Characters

*M*ANY SCIENTISTS who study animal behavior will tell you that critters don't really think or reason things out, that they're only capable of acting on instinct. Those same scientists also maintain that folks are just being overly sentimental when they attribute characteristics of personality to their animals.

Anyone who's ever worked closely with horses and mules knows that those scientists need to take a lot closer look at the evidence before making such claims. Not only do horses and mules have minds of their own, many of them possess—and demonstrate—a sense of humor as well.

The collection of stories and anecdotes in this chapter, which describe memorable personalities or recall amusing mishaps, are guaranteed to bring a few chuckles. Enjoy!

A.M. Wettach

Runaway Team Beats Urban Stress

By John H. Cunningham, Atlanta, Georgia

R ECALLING A ROUGH RIDE I survived as a country boy now provides the laughs I need to steer clear of stresses in the city's "fast lane". Modern obstacles seem small when I remember the ruts, rocks, trees and stumps we went hurtling past as I tried to regain control of a runaway team of mules.

Back before tractors were common in rural Georgia, little brother Charles and I were taking a team and wagon for a load of wood. In the mid-1930's I was only 12 and eager to help on our farm east of Lawrenceville.

At times my zeal exceeded my abilities. Before heading out after the wood I cobbled a rough—*very* rough—repair job

---

"*I* was about to get a lesson in the meaning of 'breakneck speed'..."

---

on the wagon bed. Little did I realize that my slipshod carpentry was about to give me a lesson in the meaning of "breakneck speed".

Charles and I set off rumbling down the dirt road. The wagon box bounced so hard that the boards I'd pounded into place started coming loose. I wasn't worried, however, since we'd be taking it slow.

We reached the top of a steep hill. Charles braced a stick between two spokes of a rear wheel to keep the wheel from turning...and to keep us from rolling too fast.

Broken Board Startled Mule

All went well until Charles's stick slipped, the wheel started turning, and the wagon picked up speed. Then a board broke loose at one end, swung forward and struck a mule in the rump. The mule bolted, taking its teammate, the wagon, my brother and me along with it!

The type of harness we used did not have a britching, the rump strap that would have kept the harness from sliding forward. As we raced along, the harness kept "riding up" until the collars were slipping over the mules' heads.

Boards I hadn't nailed securely were jostled loose and flew off the wagon. I bounced along on the frame as the wagon fell to pieces beneath me.

Charles leaped off the wagon and went tumbling beside the road. I dropped the right line and, with both hands, pulled hard on the left, trying to swing the mules and bring them to a stop.

ORNERY MULES sometimes gave drivers the ride of a lifetime!

The mules slowed just a little and turned into the woods. Then the left rear wheel hit a tree and snapped the coupling pole, which holds the two sets of wheels together.

Now I was riding just the frame and front wheels! The mules banged into another tree and headed up a hill. I hung on desperately as visions of Roman chariot races tore through my head.

Tired Team Came to Halt

Since the wagon was no longer poking them from behind and they were tiring on an uphill run, the mules finally began to slow. I eventually coaxed them to a stop.

They were breathing hard, stomping their hooves and tossing their heads. My legs were weak and trembling as I stepped off the remains of the wagon.

Fortunately, neither my brother, the mules nor I were injured. When the mules cooled down, I unhitched them from the broken wagon and led them back to the house.

A neighbor working in a nearby field had heard and seen the entire episode. To this day, I still grin when I recall his wry observation.

"You have all the makings of a great mule skinner," he said.

Barbed-Wire Fence Couldn't Contain Free-Spirited Mules

By Alice Schumacher, Great Falls, Montana

DAD FARMED with horses on our Oregon homestead for years but eventually acquired the team of his dream—mules. They thrived on hard work and long days in the hot sun.

But mules had their drawbacks. Fences couldn't contain them. Those sleek, long-eared beauties could ease through four strands of barbed wire without a scratch.

They terrified my mother and frequently chased her around the barnyard. She would take refuge in the wellhouse, and always claimed that they peeked at her through the knotholes as she shouted for me to come shoo the mischievous critters away.

Sometimes the mules were completely unmanageable, even for Dad. One day he drove them to Madras, our county seat, hitched to the wagon. Instead of walking obediently down Main Street, they fought the reins and went careening the length of the board sidewalks, with Dad and wagon in tow.

This display, combined with the mules' horrendous braying, attracted a crowd. When Dad finally got them turned, he headed straight for home. He was too embarrassed to ever take them to town again.

Mule's Craving Cost Grandpa

By Hazel L. Boettcher, Waller, Texas

A DECEPTIVE MULE named "Kate" cost Grandpa some money, as well as more than a little pride.

Back in the 1930's, Grandpa kept Kate as long as he could, until pressure from neighbors—who were irritated by her very unique bad habit—forced him to part with her.

He hated to do it, because Kate was a mighty fine worker, despite her treachery.

What was her sinister secret? In the dark of each early morning, Kate would open the barn gate and head to town. She'd arrive just after the bread man made a delivery to the grocery story.

All the bread was kept in a latched box, which Kate could open and close as easily as the bread man or grocer. She dearly loved the taste of fresh-baked bread and would polish off several loaves before returning home, usually before daylight.

She was eventually found out, however, and the storekeeper complained about his bread losses, as did all the folks who'd been unable to buy fresh bread due to Kate's thievery. Finally, Grandpa gave in and sold the tricky, talented mule.

About 6 months later a man came by selling mules and Grandpa bought a replacement for Kate. He chose the replacement because she was the same size and color as Kate and he hoped she'd be just as good a worker but without Kate's larcenous habits.

All went well for a few days. Then the grocer complained again of someone stealing all his bread.

Grandpa went back to the barn for a closer look at the replacement animal. Sure enough, he'd bought Kate back, and for more money than he'd sold her!

'Molly' Kept Girl from Making Mistake

By Helen Akins, Berkshire, New York

OUR MULE "MOLLY" may have kept me out of trouble once when I was a little girl.

Molly refused to take me to a spot where I wanted to pick flowers. Maybe the mule knew I hadn't asked permission from the person who planted them.

Molly was a mule my grandparents hitched with a horse named "Duke" to work on their New York farm. My mother died when I was young and my grandparents raised me.

I had an uncle who was only a year older than I. At times we were allowed to ride the hitch. We'd only ever ridden them together.

One day I spotted a patch of flowers while walking home from church. I decided to try riding Molly back to pick them.

Old Molly just wasn't the same easy-riding mule she was when riding along with Duke. I had such a hard time just getting her to the house that Grandma came out to help me get Molly going.

A.M. Wettach

GOOD COMPANIONS. Farm kids often rode gentle mules and draft horses after a day's work.

A short while later Molly stopped at the base of a steep hill and refused to move forward. Each time I tried to move her, Molly turned toward the house. Eventually I gave in and Molly trotted back home.

To this day I'll never know whether Molly was trying to keep me out of trouble or if she just missed her handsome partner, Duke.

'Dot' Sat Down to Beat the Heat

By Marty Needham, Paragould, Arkansas

SMART MULES are able to make men look a little foolish if they don't pay attention to the animals' needs. One day my father was left standing in the stirrups with his feet touching the ground. Dad's mule, "Dot", staged a sit-down strike because Dad hadn't taken time to give her a rest.

Dad often used Dot when he was hunting in the Ozark Mountains. It was kind of hot one fall day, but Dad was so intent on hunting he forgot to let Dot take a break.

Eventually she stopped and sat right down in her tracks. She wouldn't move for about 15 minutes until she had cooled down.

Some people think mules are stubborn, but I think they are just smart. They sure know how to take care of themselves!

"**'SPEED'** was a real expert at resting up during breaks!" writes Rosemary King of Milton-Freewater, Oregon. Shown here with his teammate, "Dollie", the mule would sit the entire time the men were eating dinner, Rosemary recalls. "Speed and Dollie were one of our best teams, and could work when a tractor couldn't," she adds. They were photographed in 1957 on the ranch owned by Rosemary and her husband, Dennis.

Dad's Perfect Pair

By Mrs. H. E. Smith, Clinton, Iowa

FATHER always claimed our horses, "Bill" and "Kate", were the perfect team—Kate wanted to do all the work and Bill wanted to let her!

Soldier Credited for Teamwork

By Floyd Mertz, Hecla, South Dakota

*M*Y SERVICE RECORDS show that the military must have considered "horse sense" to be a valuable commodity.

Upon induction I followed orders and made a list of all my work experience. I wrote that I could drive cars, tractors and a team of six horses—when I was a teenager in the 1930's, Dad had taught me to drive horses for planting our corn.

When I finished my hitch 4 years later, my classes and qualifications were listed on my discharge papers. Sure enough, the army included the line, "Drives six horses".

Horse Drank Like Chicken

By Harry J. Steiner, Bellaire, Michigan

A HORSE NAMED "JIM" could kill time in more ways than any other animal we ever owned. It's hard to hold back a chuckle whenever I get a mental picture of one of Jim's most entertaining tactics.

We'd always water the horses after dinner and Jim would stand at the trough and drink just like a chicken.

Jim would just touch his lips to the water and slurp out a mouthful. Then he'd hold his head high in the air and let gravity send the water down his long throat.

Jim would drink like this, one mouthful at a time, until someone led him away from the trough. We were convinced he drank this way just to delay going back to work.

One afternoon when we finally got Jim back on the job, we had quite a time. I was walking with the plow behind Jim and "Bess" when we hit a big alfalfa root.

I was holding the plow handles with both hands. The lines were tied together around my waist.

The plow hit the tough root and stuck. Before I could yell

"whoa" or get free of the lines, the team pulled me right over the plow handles.

I got a face-first ride for quite a ways along the edge of the furrow before I could get the team stopped. Luckily, nothing more than my pride was hurt!

Deaf Horse Taught Farmer The Value of Listening

By Alton Peterson, Osakis, Minnesota

A NEIGHBOR WHO WOULDN'T listen once was taught a lesson by our deaf horse, "King".

It's funny now. But back then it cost our neighbor a wagon, a harness and a bit of his pride.

I had to sell our team of horses in 1946 when we moved from Preston to a larger farm near Lanesboro in southeastern Minnesota. King and "Bud" seemed like excellent animals for Walter Mills, an elderly neighbor who needed a team for farm chores.

Walter liked King and Bud but didn't listen to a warning about driving the team. I told him to keep a hold of the lines because King was deaf and couldn't respond to voice commands.

I'd learned this the hard way while trying to teach King his first work routine on our farm. Usually I would open a gate and send the team through on voice commands.

As the horses cleared the opening I would "whoa" them to a stop while I closed the gate. I was in for a surprise when I tried that with King.

King kept going, no matter how hard I hollered or Bud tried to stop. I had to chase after the lines to get them stopped.

King Failed Firecracker Test

My suspicions about King's deafness were confirmed later. I tossed a couple of firecrackers out in the pasture where the horses were grazing.

Bud bucked, snorted and fled from the noises. King kept

his nose buried in the lush grass. He hadn't heard a thing.

As I tried to recount these stories to Walter, he acted a bit hard of hearing himself. Walter just said that King couldn't match wits with a horseman of his experience.

He said he intended to break King of his bad habit and teach him the meaning of the word *"WHOA!"*

Two months later I saw Walter's hired hand trying to avoid me at a sale. But after a lot of persuading he finally told me

> *"King and Bud ran into the woods, the wagon clattering along behind..."*

about Walter's experience with King and Bud.

Walter and his hired man were mending fence. Walter was going to allow the team to walk on its own, commanding them to stop at each post.

Soon enough, Walter hollered for the team to stop. Bud tried but King kept going.

Walter continued to holler as the team walked by the first four fence posts. Walter and his hired man spooked the animals when they ran after them.

King and Bud ran into the woods, with the wagon full of fencing equipment clattering along behind. The horses raced through the trees and down a steep bluff. By the time Walter and his hired man got there, the harness and wagon were wrecked.

Fortunately, King and Bud weren't injured. Walter sold the team and swore the hired hand to silence.

Never again was Walter willing to talk horses with me.

Cold Cured Mule of Fooling Farmer

By Fanny Miller, Anderson County, South Carolina

ONCE IN AWHILE, a mule could be too smart for his own good. Dad got the last laugh on "Ben" when the mule became stubborn late one cold winter day. Ben refused to go in the barn when Dad attempted to put him up for the night.

Instead of following Dad's usual instructions, Ben kept dodging and running around a straw stack. Dad didn't waste much time on Ben's antics.

Dad slammed the barn door shut and left Ben out all night. The next day Ben was at the door, ready to come in. Ben never tried that trick on Dad again.

That didn't stop Ben from pulling tricks on other people, however. Ben and his partner "Jack" always seemed to know when they were being driven by an inexperienced hand.

One day Ben began limping while he and Jack were pulling a harrow. Ben's condition seemed so severe that the new driver unhitched the mule.

As soon as Ben was free he kicked up his heels and ran for the barn.

"'**OL' GRADY**' was my favorite animal on the farm, and also the favorite of the rest of the family," writes Ernest Wester of Smyrna, Georgia in recalling the gray mule shown with Ernest's father in this photo. "Grady was always a dependable worker, whether snaking logs out of new ground or pulling a 1,300-pound wagonload of cotton to the gin. We kids always had serious 'discussions' to determine who got to ride Grady to and from the fields at mealtimes!"

Time to Go!

By Opal Cavanah, Dixon, Kentucky

*I*N WEBSTER COUNTY, Kentucky during the winters of the 1930's, my father drove a covered wagon, heated with a small kerosene stove, that carried about 25 students to school. Depending on the condition of the roads, he'd sometimes use as many as four horses.

One cold afternoon, he started out from home a bit early and decided to stop for coffee at the little cafe in town. When he came out a short time later, the horses and wagon were gone!

Father ran to the schoolhouse, about half a mile away. Sure enough, there they were. Not only had the horses realized it was time to pick up the children, but upon arriving at the school they had also turned around to be in the exact spot Father always drove them to for the children to climb aboard!

Green Mules? Wow!

By Jason Hertzler, Milton, Pennsylvania

*W*HEN I was a boy, we lived on a small farm in Cumberland County, Pennsylvania and farmed with three horses. In adjacent York County, my Grandfather Burkhart farmed with six mules. I loved those mules!

My uncle would get them ready for the field, and they'd stand there looking so sharp and intelligent. They always walked so gracefully and seemed willing to work. I longed for the day we could have a team of mules.

One fall I heard that Grandpa had purchased a new team of "green" mules. I could hardly wait to see them. You can imagine my surprise when I finally did see them, only to discover that green didn't refer to their color, but the fact that they weren't yet trained for work!

We moved to a larger farm a short time later, and I begged

Daddy for a pair of mules. At first he said we couldn't afford them, but 3 years later, we got our first team. I was really proud of them because mules were rare in Cumberland County.

Their names were "Tom" and "Jerry", and they were well-trained. Jerry was the leader, and he had a very special characteristic. When you told him to "Giddap!", he'd always (and I mean always!) nod his head before starting. It was his signal to us and to Tom that he was ready to go.

Tom would occasionally balk if he thought a load was too heavy. Jerry would reach across and nip Tom on the neck, and then Tom would really tear into it. After a while, all Jerry had to do was *pretend* to bite Tom, and Tom would buckle down and start pulling.

Writing about Tom and Jerry brings back lots of happy memories. One final story I'd like to share: I heard of an old character who always cussed at his mules when he worked them. Then he was converted, and after he started talking like a Christian should, his mules were confused and he had to retrain them!

'Sandy' Is Still Special

By Madge M. Schultz, Billings, Montana

SEVENTY YEARS of ranch life still haven't been long enough for me to find a replacement for "Sandy".

The beautiful sorrel gelding was the best of the good horses we used on our ranches in eastern Montana. Sandy's hardworking attitude and faithful devotion to us earned him a special chapter in my book of memories.

Uncle Mac went to the Miles City sale in 1918 and bought Sandy from a group of unbroken 3-year-olds. Sandy was a quick learner and soon became a favorite on Uncle Mac's ranch on Rosebud Creek.

I met Sandy when we went there in 1921 to help my ailing uncle. Mother was so busy cleaning, cooking and taking care of Uncle Mac that I got to spend more time with Father.

That meant more time with Sandy, too. Sandy was hitched with "Nip". Nip never did care for the attention from a little girl, but Sandy always enjoyed my affection.

When we went to feed cattle Dad would lift me up to pet Sandy. Through that stroking and nuzzling we began to de-

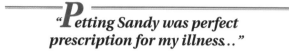

"*Petting Sandy was perfect prescription for my illness.."*

velop a special relationship.

Later I realized that people's and animal's feelings for one another can be powerful medicine. When I was quite ill one summer, Dad led Sandy up to the house.

Petting Perked up Sick Girl

Dad hoisted me up on Sandy's back so I could pet him. That was the perfect prescription for my illness. In short order I was my usual perky self.

Sandy once nuzzled Nip's face and neck, trying to perk up his hitch partner as Nip recovered from a leg injury. After

"'SILVERTON' AND 'DU-RANGO' are semi-retired logging mules from Tennessee," writes Gene Corrigan of LaPryor, Texas. "They're both in their 20's, very gentle, with loads of personality and still like to work," he says. A conductor on the Silverton train, Gene gave the mules their current names because he didn't know what they'd been called originally—and because he wanted something with a western flavor to correspond to their new home!

watching Nip just walk off, I wasn't sure he was worthy of Sandy's affection.

I was overjoyed later when Uncle Mac gave Sandy to us. He said he wanted to be sure Sandy always had a good home.

When I was old enough to drive, I used Sandy and Nip to mow, rake and stack hay. Often I rode Sandy home from the hay fields.

The end came quickly for Sandy during the spring of 1937. He'd spent a leisurely winter enjoying good grain and hay he had helped harvest the summer before.

That spring morning Sandy had gone to the creek for a drink. On his way back to the barn, he suddenly collapsed.

I'm happy Sandy didn't suffer. And I'm thankful for all the wonderful memories he left me of our time together.

His Pal 'Rock'

By Ivan Pfalser, Caney, Kansas

THE LAST TEAM my dad, John Pfalser, farmed with was a pair of Belgian-Percheron cross geldings named "Barney" and "Rock". Barney was black, and Rock was brown. Both had white blazes. In their prime, the pair weighed just over 2 tons.

At the time, in the late 1930's and early '40's, our family farmed in north-central Oklahoma and then south-central Kansas. Barney and Rock had worked together most of their lives with Dad behind them. He always said if those two were hitched to a load and they couldn't move it, nothing could.

Dad sold Barney in 1938 and always regretted it, so Rock became a permanent fixture on our farm. I even learned to ride him. Of course, his back was so broad that my legs stuck straight out sideways!

Once in a great while, I could get him to gallop, but then I'd usually lose my balance and fall off. When this happened, Rock would immediately stop and look around to see if I was hurt.

He was very patient about waiting for me to climb back on him, then he'd start out again at a slower pace. He knew better than I did how fast we should travel!

One year we were cutting field cane to be used for silage. The cane was loaded onto hayracks as high as the men could pitch it, and a tractor pulled several loaded wagons to the pit silo where the cane was ground.

Dad used Rock to pull each loaded wagon up to the ensilage cutter. Once, after Rock was hooked to the lead wagon, he laid into the leathers but nothing moved. He slacked off and tried again, and the wagon moved very slowly. Then someone yelled "Whoa!"

They had forgotten to unhook the second loaded wagon from the first. Rock had moved them both!

Dad said Rock could outpull any two-horse team in the county. Alone, he could pull out any vehicle stuck in an Oklahoma red-dirt mud hole.

Rock lived to be about 30 years old, and his final years were

"'PRINCE' would always lift his foreleg when you asked him to shake hands," writes Kevin Thomas of Milwaukee, Wisconsin. "My grandfather, Fred Voss (shown here at age 14), said Prince was an excellent lead horse and very intelligent—he could untie ropes and open barn doors!"

pretty easy ones. The last few times he was in harness, I used him to pull a two-section harrow to bust down lister rows in a field of young corn. He could walk all the way down a 2,000-foot row and never touch a single plant!

Mare Made Trip a Lifelong Memory

By Josh Ramey, Elizabeth, Colorado

I STILL HAVE warm memories of the clippity-clop of "Kit's" hooves on the paved road as she took us to school. Kit was one of the horses essential to our existence in northwest Kansas during the "Dirty Thirties". She had a lot of jobs around the farm.

As far as my brother and I were concerned, none was more important than taking us to school. This may have been one of Kit's favorite jobs too. My brother and I were a lot lighter than Kit's normal loads.

Kit usually was hitched with "Star". The large Percherons hauled hay to our cattle during the winter.

Mother Made Lunches

Each morning before harnessing the team for work, Dad would get Kit ready to take us to grade school. While Dad gave Kit her grain, Mother was busy in the kitchen.

After making jelly sandwiches, she'd pack them with hard-boiled eggs and apples in an old gallon maple syrup pail. We

> *"Mother handed up our syrup pail and Kit would walk to school..."*

thought we had really great lunches, especially for those tough days.

By the time Mother had finished, we were ready for the trip to school. Dad and Kit would be waiting at the front door to start us off.

Dad would lift my brother up on Kit and put me up behind him. Mother would hand up the syrup pail and Kit would walk off, headed for school.

I can still see us now. Kit's back was so broad that as she walked along our little legs stuck straight out to the sides.

Kit wore her work bridle and my brother held the reins. He never did much with them because Kit just went along at a nice pace, needing no guidance.

When we arrived at school we'd slide off Kit's back. The kind mare would turn and trot for home, where she'd rejoin Dad and put in a full day in the field.

Some horses you never forget, and Old Kit is certainly in that category.

He Wasn't Worth Beans

By Raymond Pait, Ben Wheeler, Texas

ONE YEAR in the midst of the growing season, Dad's only workhorse was bitten by a snake and died.

That was during the Depression, and Dad didn't have enough money to buy another horse. So we went looking for a mule, hoping we could find one cheap. We finally did, but it looked so bad, Dad almost didn't buy him.

He was covered with dark blotches and scruffy hair, and Dad thought he had the mange. The owner said the mule had been burned in a fire but otherwise was okay.

Having no choice, Dad bought the mule. Because he was afraid the mule wouldn't be worth beans, we named him "Beans".

After we got Beans home, it began to appear that Dad had gotten a bargain! Beans was a hard, steady worker who was also gentle and very smart. You only had to show him how to do something once…after that, he'd do it on his own.

He never stepped on the tobacco plants and would haul a load of ripe leaves into the barn completely by himself. There was only one problem—if Beans spotted a fire, he would panic. Then you never knew what damage he might do.

Even an open firebox on a passing locomotive could cause

him to run away, maybe trampling a crop or breaking a piece of equipment in the process.

Dad soon wondered whether it was worth having Beans around. Mom pointed out that we *needed* Beans, adding that the mule couldn't help being afraid of fire.

Then one night there was a fire in the barn. Beans made such a ruckus breaking out that it woke up everyone in time to save the barn and all the tobacco hanging inside.

When the fire was out, Beans came walking slowly back to the house. Dad was so grateful that Beans' commotion had saved an entire harvest that he vowed never to sell the scruffy-looking mule.

Beans never did get over his fear of fire...and Dad never could keep from losing his temper when Beans ran away. But from then on, Dad said Beans was the smartest work animal he ever had!

Mules Made Mess of Hay Stack

By Bernice Begalka, Ellensburg, Washington

OUR SNEAKY MULES made me feel mighty incompetent when I tried to help Dad make hay.

During World War II, I had to help Dad and the neighbors with fieldwork. A lot of the boys, including my five brothers, were away in the service.

We worked our Washington farm with mules. Dad said they were more dependable, stronger and smarter than horses. They sure always managed to outsmart me.

Another man said that when mules were going to try to trick you, they'd work at it a little at a time. They figured if they did something gradually, a man wouldn't notice what they were trying to get away with. After my childhood experiences, I believe he was onto something.

Dad drove a team pulling the bucker, which brought the hay to the stacker. I drove the pull-up team, which was supposed to be an easy job.

I would drive the mules straight away as they pulled on a rope. It went up through a pulley and would lift the hay up and dump it on the stack.

One Step Short

For awhile the mules would go the right distance and everything would work well. Then they would stop one step short of the exact distance needed. On the next load they would stop another step shorter.

They would do this until I caught them and tried to make them quit or until they'd dumped the load short of the hay stack.

That would delay their work while the men had to pick up all the spilled hay. I tried for three seasons, but I never did have the authority or the smarts to keep those mules from periodically playing tricks on me and dropping hay all over the place.

Mule Brayed at Horses

By Dick Pengilly, Lafayette, Minnesota

THE MULES we used for odd jobs and light fieldwork were a handy size—1,000 to 1,200 pounds.

One was named "Tom". He was good-natured, and one day on the spur of the moment I decided to see if he could be ridden. I led him into a freshly plowed field where the dirt was soft and got on.

He performed like a trooper, so after that I rode him a lot. My wife and I belonged to a saddle club, and one time I took Tom on a trail ride.

When we came to a dry creek bed, Tom refused to cross. You should have heard all the jokes about a stubborn mule and how I should get a horse.

Then one of the folks on a horse went around me and into the dry creek bed. Immediately the horse sank into soft sand up to his belly!

Without any direction from me, Tom turned and went down

the creek about 100 feet and crossed there. The sand was so hard he hardly made any tracks.

To my eye, there was no difference between the two crossings, but Tom knew that one was safe and the other wasn't. Once on the other side, Tom looked upstream at the horses still struggling through the sand and let out a bray you had to hear to believe.

I'll leave it to your imagination what Tom was saying to those horses and their riders…but I reckon I agreed with him!

'Melvin' Made Dad's Life Interesting

By Faye Buice, Suwanee, Georgia

OUR MULE "MELVIN" must have had a strange sense of humor, according to Dad's recollection.

Sometimes Melvin made my Dad so angry I wondered how they ever worked together. Melvin seemed to provoke Dad just for amusement.

One time Melvin came so close to running the wagon into a train that Dad nearly jumped for his life. This all started when Dad hitched up Melvin for an ordinary trip to the nearby town of Oakwood.

About a mile from town a bird flew across the road in front of Melvin. The mule made the most of this opportunity to spook and raced off at a full gallop, with the wagon clattering along behind.

The fast ride was dangerous enough. Then Dad heard a train's whistle. It was chugging at a good clip toward the crossing they were both approaching.

For a few tense seconds Dad didn't think he had any more chance of stopping that stubborn mule than the engineer did of stopping his speeding train.

Dad was fighting for control of Melvin. He finally decided the war was lost and prepared to jump for his life.

An instant before Dad was about to jump, Melvin skidded to a stop as the train rushed by. Melvin was so close to the tracks that if he hadn't turned his head the train would've taken it off.

Dad's Decision Backfired

Another day, just to see if he could get the best of Melvin in a more controlled situation, Dad decided to try to ride the mule while inside the barn. He figured Melvin would realize that, because he was completely enclosed by the barn's four walls, he'd have to behave in a docile manner.

Wrong! Melvin went wild as soon as Dad slipped up on his back. Melvin immediately tried to slam Dad against the stall supports and nearly bucked him into the ceiling.

Dad kept a good grip as Melvin almost turned himself inside out bucking. Finally Dad lost his hold and hit the floor. He looked like he'd gone 20 rounds with a wildcat and lost.

Dad did say later that Melvin was very good at some things around the farm. He was good at eating, balking at work and—most of all—figuring out ways to drive Dad crazy.

Mule Helped Friends

By Harriett Green, Plano, Iowa

WE HAD a mule named "Joker" who was small in size but big in smarts.

We bought him from a neighbor who couldn't keep him from opening gates and wandering off. Our place was one of Joker's regular stops when he got out, and that's how we got to know him.

We figured the reason Joker escaped so often was that he was lonely. So when we bought him, we put him in with our horses.

After that, he usually stayed put, apparently happy with his new friends. Occasionally, however, he'd open the gate or jump the fence, probably just to show he could come and go as he pleased.

One day during a dry spell, Joker got out and came walking up to the house. When I went to see what he was up to, he

Erwin "Bud" Nielsen

MULES AND HORSES were often teamed together by innovative farmers needing maximum horsepower.

turned around and headed back to the horse pasture.

I followed him and soon discovered that the stock tank in the pasture was bone-dry. I filled it with water and left Joker and the horses happily quenching their thirst.

After that, whenever the water in the tank was low, Joker came up to the house to get me. There's no doubt in my mind that he was just making sure his friends the horses had all the water they needed.

There's nothing like a mule for good "horse sense"!

'Jim' and 'Slim'

By Robert Knott, Lacrosse, Washington

WHEN COULEE DAM was under construction, our family was farming in the Palouse region of Washington State. We had about 50 mules and ran four 10-mule teams.

One year we needed a few more head and heard about a farmer near Coulee Dam, about 130 miles away, who had six mules for sale.

We drove over and bought them. In those days, there wasn't a good way to haul livestock around, so I led the mules home on horseback, taking 4 days to get there.

I worked two of those mules as a team that fall and again the following spring. Their names were "Jim" and "Slim". They were a good hardworking team with common sense.

But when we turned them onto pasture the following summer, they disappeared. After looking high and low, we figured they'd jumped the fence and headed for their old home.

When we got some slack time, we drove back up to Coulee Dam. There we met a man who was dealing in both mules and horses.

He said he'd recently seen two mules just like Jim and Slim in the rugged Columbia River country. He offered to trade us a pretty decent horse for those two runaway mules. We accepted the offer…it was a lot better than going home empty-handed.

That fellow just waited till there were 10 or 12 inches of snow on the ground. Then Jim and Slim came looking for a good feed bag and a barn to sleep in.

I always wished we'd gotten Jim and Slim back…it was fun working with such a spirited pair. I hope they're doing well in "mule heaven"!

'Tom' Knew When to Turn

By Maurice Robertson, Eagle, Nebraska

*P*ICKING CORN was an opportunity for our old mule "Tom" to show how smart he was.

I had Tom when we started farming in Nebraska in 1937. After picking a couple rows of corn, Tom always seemed to know right where to turn without damaging our crops.

I used Tom and three 2-year-old horses to work our fields. That mule was the best animal we ever had for breaking colts.

Tom also was stronger than our horses. I would work our horses half a day. Old Tom would work all day long, every day.

The mules got along well with the horses. Our mules were fond of cattle, too.

One of Father's mules saw a newborn calf that had gotten on the wrong side of a fence. The mule used its teeth to pick the calf up and gently set it on the right side of the fence.

The calf might not have lived had it not been able to get back to the cow.

'Babe' and 'Barney'

By Jan Roat, Red Lodge, Montana

BACK IN THE 1940's, Daddy worked for a man who raised horses. When one of the foals—a Clydesdale—was born blind, the boss wanted to put it down.

Daddy talked the boss into giving him the little filly instead. He named her "Babe". She had keen hearing and smell, and quickly learned to follow the sound of Daddy's voice.

When Babe was old enough, Daddy easily broke her to harness. Then he bought a half-Percheron, half-Clydesdale named "Barney".

Barney was huge! Daddy was 6 feet tall and always wore a striped railroad cap, but even so, he could stand up straight under Barney's head.

Daddy got a contract to mow weeds along the railroad track with Babe and Barney. The weeds were taller than Daddy, so he'd walk ahead checking for rocks, then call for Babe and Barney to follow.

One day, a train came clanging by. After it was gone, Daddy called for Babe and Barney, but nothing happened.

He rushed back through the weeds, and there was Barney, lying on the ground. Daddy knelt down, afraid the big horse was dead.

But he wasn't. It turned out that every time a train passed, Barney would lie down and play dead!

There probably aren't many folks who'd want a team with one blind horse and another that lies down when a train passes…but Babe and Barney were mighty special, especially after you got to know them well!

'Sophie's' Sweet Tooth Made Her a Favorite

By James S. McLellan, Greenville, Maine

STRAWBERRY SODA was the drink that hit the spot for "Sophie" after a day working in our fields.

Of all the horses we ever owned for farming in Maine, Sophie was most memorable. That's probably because Uncle Walter taught Sophie to drink from a bottle.

Sophie was a dappled chestnut mare on our best team. Sophie was so smart it didn't take long for Uncle Walter to teach her anything.

Uncle Walter would put a bottle between Sophie's lips.

"After working up a sweat Sophie loved a soda..."

She would hold it steady, tilt her head back and guzzle down the strawberry soda.

Sophie was fond of the attention. And after working up a sweat, she sure loved the strawberry soda.

Sophie was one of the best horses we ever had. "Barney", on the other hand, was one of the worst.

Weighing over a ton, Barney was the largest horse we ever owned. With all that weight, when Barney balked on a job he was impossible to move.

Barney's partner was "Prince". Clomping along at over 5-miles-per-hour, they were the fastest team we had.

'Barney' Best at Easy Jobs

They were great at mowing, which required little effort. They worked fine on any job that didn't require much effort.

That's because Barney would stop long before any sweat began to show up on his shoulders. Barney didn't kick, plunge or lie down. He simply refused to move. No effort would budge Barney until the load was lightened.

With this behavior, Barney began to deplete Dad's abundant supply of patience. When it had been entirely exhausted, Barney was sold and went off to work where the demands weren't so rigorous.

'Don' and 'Dan' Damaged Most Machinery

Our most handsome team was "Don" and "Dan", a pair of chestnuts. They were ideal for working in the woods, using simple, cheap, durable equipment, such as stone boats and sleds.

The trouble was, Don and Dan wrecked more expensive equipment than all of our other horses combined. They ran off with a hay wagon, a grain binder and a drill seeder.

The last victim of their abuse was a land roller. The team bolted, jerking the lines from my uncle's hands.

Racing across the yard, each horse picked a different side of an elm tree to pass. The pole between the horses hit the tree dead center.

The pole broke in three pieces. The neck yoke shattered. Bits of leather and broken buckles flew everywhere.

RAMBUNCTIOUS CHESTNUTS "Don" and "Dan" (above) proved to be a bit too costly for farmer to keep!

The horses stopped a few yards later. They started to graze as though nothing had happened.

After that episode, Don and Dan became the down payment on the tractor Dad had been considering buying.

Cooperative Horses Much Appreciated

By Merle Hasenclever, Fort Madison, Iowa

HARVESTING HAY on our Iowa farm was made a lot easier because of our talented team of horses.

"Jim" and "Bob" really knew how to make my life

easier while working in the field. Their cooperation allowed me to concentrate all my efforts on building big loads of hay.

Back during the 1940's some of those loads would weigh a ton or more when we finished. I was able to maintain this production because of Jim, a gray horse, and Bob, a black one.

They weren't as large as other draft horses in the area, but their intelligence and energy compensated for what they lacked in size.

Jim and Bob couldn't wait to get going when they were hitched to a heavy load. They could move any load and would pull until told to stop.

While haying, the team would straddle a row pulling a wagon to which we attached a hay loader. They would walk the rectangular field, turning the corners on their own at just the right spot without instructions from anyone.

Believe me, those qualities in workhorses were really appreciated by busy farmers.

Horses Worked Without a Driver

By Elmer D. Lapp, Kinzers, Pennsylvania

ONE TEAM I had was so good, the horses would work on their own.

One day while disking I had to help unload bags of seed being delivered. I wrapped the lines around the disk lever and left "Lady", "Barb", "Shirley" and "Jean".

When I returned they were gone. I scanned the field and found them disking on their own.

That team was so dependable I trusted them to disk with my 7-year-old son driving.

They worked so well they would pull anything anywhere I asked. Once they pulled a fuel truck free from muddy ruts on a steep grade.

Another time a neighbor's tractor couldn't move a log. He laughed when I hitched Lady and Barb to the huge, stubborn piece of timber.

FOUR-HORSE TEAM was so dependable they could be handled by 7-year-old (above) or even disk a field without a driver!

He stopped laughing and thanked me when they left that log right where he wanted it.

In 1954 I added "Polly" and "Molly" to the team. With the six-horse hitch and using only one line, I drove a Conestoga wagon from Lancaster, Pennsylvania to Wheeling, West Virginia.

I made the trip to commemorate the 250th anniversary of using wagons to haul freight from Philadelphia to Wheeling.

'Snip' Stood Waiting for Teammate

By Richard Bott, Munith, Michigan

OUR MARE "SNIP" standing near a rake waiting to work is one of my warmest memories of growing up on a Michigan farm.

The smart little mare was just a joy to work with. One morning I bridled Snip and let her walk to the water tank on her own.

I went to get "Dora", Snip's teammate, and when I returned Snip was gone. Early morning darkness made searching difficult. After 20 minutes I walked out to the edge of a field where we'd raked beans the day before.

There stood Snip. She was standing on her side of the tongue on the rake she'd pulled the day before.

Snip had gotten her drink. Now she was waiting patiently for Dora and I so we could get to work.

Another time I teamed Snip with "Maude" to clean out a shallow ditch. First we plowed three furrows in the ditch. Then we dragged a board scraper through to clean it out.

Plowing had left a hard collar on the edge of each furrow. Snip was such a hard worker and she increased her efforts so much at each hard spot that she almost pulled me over the plow handles.

Old Mare Kept Colt Trotting

Snip often liked to trot while working. I remember Snip still trotting when she was 23 years old and I was driving her with colt.

Maude usually was hitched with her full sister, "Kit". The black mares were full of spirit and could be counted to run off

"We were dragged through a long stretch of water..."

with a piece of equipment at least once a year.

They gave my brother, Arthur, and me a real wet ride one spring day. Kit was grazing and lifted her head. It was under the neck yoke, which raised and startled Kit.

As they bolted, Arthur grabbed Maude's bridle and hame and I grabbed for the same on Kit. We were dragged along as fast as they could go through a long, splashy stretch of water.

Were we wet and muddy when they finally came to a stop! I'll never know whether we stopped them or if they were just too tired to keep running.

Later in life I was better equipped to chase after them. One day my wife, Bertha, had driven our new car over to visit while I cultivated corn.

When Bertha wanted to leave I had to turn the car around for her. As soon as I started the car Maude and Kit started for home. I drove right along behind them.

Most of the time these horses would stay for hours in the spots we'd left them. We just never knew when they would take off!

'Star' Got Good Grades from Farmer

By Harold Buswell, Ipava, Illinois

OUR MARE "Star" was aptly named—she was so smart she should have taught horse sense to our other work animals.

She knew where to find cool water and could tell time. She would even look for Dad to doctor an injury rather than run away from the necessary treatment.

The beautiful mare still stands tall in my memories of growing up on a farm in Missouri. I was the youngest son in a family of seven boys and five girls.

We boys all worked alongside Dad in the fields and around the barn. Being the youngest, I was assigned to remove the harnesses from our mules and horses and to feed and water the animals.

Star Found Cooler Water

I got a good look at Star's intelligent behavior every day. At first I wondered why Star buried her head almost up to her eyes while drinking from the stock tank.

One day I plunged my arm down into the water, fishing for an answer. The water at the bottom of the tank was way cooler than the sun-warmed layer at the top.

Dad said that each day just before noon, Star would turn to look at him. Dad said Star knew how to tell him she wanted her cool drink.

Star sure knew how to take care of herself. Once while Dad was working in the barn, Star limped over and held out a front hoof.

Dad examined it and found a nail stuck in the soft part of her hoof. Dad removed the nail and was rewarded with a grateful nuzzle from Star.

'Buck' Could 'Towel' Time

By Jenna V. Ownbey, Amarillo, Texas

*D*RIVING A MULE when I was only 9 years old taught me how smart these animals can be.

"Buck" certainly seemed to know more about farming than I did. And I swear he could tell time.

I drove the buckskin mule as my father's only helping hand on our farm near Dalhart, Texas. When we cultivated corn, my father, Henry Stephenson, drove a four-horse rig.

It cultivated two rows on either side of the row he walked along. My job was to trail along with Buck, cultivating the row Dad missed.

Every day when it was nearly noon Buck would slow down and bray. No matter where we were he'd turn and head for the house, dragging me along behind.

Mother would hang a white dish towel from the top of the kitchen screen door when dinner was ready. I don't know if Buck saw that white towel or if he had an internal clock.

Not only are mules smart, they aren't bothered by things that affect horses. We farmed during the Dust Bowl days and all our horses eventually developed pneumonia from the dust and died.

Buck was the only one of our animals to survive. He was eventually retired to pasture where his only excitement was watching for Mother to hang out her dinner-time towel.

Mules Loved Petting

By Marjean Viksna, Sioux Falls, South Dakota

*T*HE TWO MULES "Jack" and "Jenny" always loved the attention I would give them at the end of each workday. The mules made a wonderful team for me when I helped Father with the work on our South Dakota farm back in the 1930's. Jack and Jenny loved to be petted each night when they came in for their water, oats and hay.

I drove Jack and Jenny to rake hay. The smart team kept me from stumbling in badger holes.

Jack and Jenny would rake straight along in a hay field until they saw a badger hole. Then they would walk around it, their change of course warning me of the hole.

The only trouble with Jack and Jenny was that they spooked easily. Just about anything could set them off—a bird, a car and even some people.

Sometimes when they spooked I'd get a fast ride across a hay field. I'd have to lead them back to where we left off raking and start all over again.

Precision Planter Strayed on First Job

By Dan H. Sullivan, Springfield, Missouri

*P*LANTING CORN in straight rows was a job I did so well I never thought it would be the basis for a funny story. While growing up on a farm in central Arkansas, I earned a reputation for precision planting. With a good team of horses or mules I would plant cotton, corn and other crops with a two-row drill or planter.

The first team I ever used was a gentle and obedient gray mare and an easy-going mule. They were perfect for precision planting.

Soon I was known throughout the community for the pride I took in planting straight rows. My employer began hiring me out to plant for other farmers.

I was accurate as ever on my first job off his place. But it almost tarnished my reputation.

I proceeded to plant corn, as I'd been instructed. When I finished, the rows in that 6-acre field were, as usual, straight as an arrow.

I realized something was wrong when I checked the planter and found it almost empty. I had planted seed for the whole farm on that one small field.

My face turned red when I saw the source of my problem. I'd forgotten to put the corn plate in the planter.

I had been planting cotton, using a plate for dense seeding. Corn seed, however, was supposed to be planted with a plate which spaced the larger seeds about 4 inches apart.

The farmer later told me that the rows of corn were sure straight. But he had never seen so much corn come up in so small a field!

Wasps Won Race for Farm Girl

By Emma L. Trisler, Jonesville, Louisiana

A NEST OF WASPS once helped me win a mule race on our childhood farm in Louisiana.

Some special evenings after work was done Dad let my older brother Dub and I ride two of the mules to water at a nearby river. Dub was riding "Red" and I was riding "Old Kate".

One evening we decided to race. Dub and Red were in the lead until I rode Kate under a limb hanging low with the weight of a wasps' nest.

Their stinging encouragement spurred Kate on. Needless to say, we won the race!

Dub and I are now in our late 60's. We still chuckle when we think of this race so many decades ago.

Canadian Colts Swam for New York State

By John Teefy, Ottawa, Ontario

T WO COLTS who decided to go for a swim in Lake Ontario gave their young caretakers quite a scare.

Back in 1918, we lived on a farm about 20 miles east of Toronto. One afternoon, two boys on a neighboring farm decided they'd try their hand at breaking their father's two new colts, although he'd told them not to take the untrained horses out of the barn while he went to town.

Determined to go ahead with their plan, the boys hitched the colts to an empty stone boat and drove them out onto the road. Soon the boys were enjoying their outing along the scenic shore of Lake Ontario.

They became so caught up in their adventure that they didn't notice whatever it was that spooked the horses. The young team bolted, running right for the water. The boys hung on, figuring the cold waves would turn the colts back and their worries would be over.

But as the team hit the water the stone boat stuck in the sand and the horses broke free. The colts crashed into the waves and started swimming straight south. It seemed as

> *"Father told them not to take untrained colts out of barn..."*

though they intended to take up residency in New York, about 30 miles across the icy lake!

Colts Dots on Horizon

The boys' concern turned to genuine fright. Instead of fearing the water, the young horses seemed to enjoy its cool currents. They kept swimming south for so long that their forms became only tiny dots, then eventually vanished past the horizon.

The boys waited on the beach, fearing their father's wrath more than the approaching gloom of night. When they'd hardly any hope left, the two tiny specks appeared again on the skyline.

After an agonizing wait, the colts finally swam back into clear view. The young animals seemed not to have suffered at all.

Acting totally unconcerned, the colts trotted up out of the water. They planted their feet exactly in the tracks they'd left earlier, eager to head home.

The boys followed along, though at a much slower pace. They knew their father would be waiting for them, and they weren't eager to explain the afternoon's events!

Mules Lose Hired Hand

By Marjorie Weber, Sims, Illinois

O UR HIRED MAN may not have thought this was funny at the time, but I'll bet he had a few laughs later. While cultivating corn one day our hired man blew his nose so loudly it startled the team of mules. They jumped so quickly that he took a tumble backwards off the cultivator.

The hired man landed in the field. He wasn't injured, except maybe his pride was bruised a little.

The mules ran across a half-mile field without ever damaging a single stalk of corn. Not even one strap was broken on the harness.

The mules stopped at the end of the field and browsed as my husband went to get them. The docile mules went right back to work as though nothing had ever happened.

I don't know how the hired man felt at the time. But I think that this shows mules have a sense of humor as well as having common sense.

Missouri Mule Showed Me

By Joe Wallenburg, Otterville, Missouri

A CLEVER MULE named "Tom" and a nearby rock pile gave me a hard lesson in respect.

Tom was a mule my father teamed with "Bert" for work on the family farm 3 miles north of Branson, Missouri. My younger brother, Almer, and I decided to ride the mules one day while Dad and the other men ate dinner.

The team looked like easy prey, grazing in the pasture close to the house, still in harness. Only their bridles were removed for the hour break.

The trouble was, while Bert was an easy catch, Tom always tried his best to evade us. But Almer and I devised a plan.

We caught Bert and both climbed up on his back. Then

Almer guided Bert alongside Tom and I jumped over onto Tom's back.

I wasn't on Tom long enough to grab any part of his harness. The mule headed straight for a huge rock pile and started bucking wildly.

I can still can feel those bruises as though he'd pitched me onto those rocks yesterday. Tom was a tough teacher, but his lesson about interrupting dinner breaks sure improved my manners…at least around mules!

Fed Up with Range, Horses Tried to Catch Train Home

By Lowell Larsen, Rock Springs, Wyoming

IN THE EARLY 1920's, my parents moved from eastern to western South Dakota. It was a 350-mile trip, so we shipped everything—livestock included—by train. The animals and farm equipment were unloaded in the small town of Scenic, then taken 9 miles to our homestead.

Our new farm was in the Badlands, with its bare white buttes and unimproved roads. Most of the land consisted of open range, with a few scattered farms and ranches and very few fences.

The watercourses were dry except when it rained. We had no hay or oats the first year, so the animals were turned out to graze on the range. Whenever we needed the workhorses, we had to go out and find them. It was amazing how big and empty the South Dakota Badlands were.

One morning Dad couldn't find them in their usual place—and with good reason. They had found their way back the entire 9 miles to the spot in Scenic where they'd been unloaded from the train!

The horses must have decided this no-hay, no-oats life wasn't for them and hoped someone would put them on an eastbound train back to Minnehaha County!

Horse, Driver and Rake Took a Tumble

By Robert Thompson, Kent, Washington

NICKS AND BRUISES but no broken bones were the results of a childhood accident that caused more laughs than injuries.

I was heading home after raking hay on our Wisconsin farm. I wasn't paying quite close enough attention to "Fanny" and "Queen". The hub on the left wheel hit a gate post, setting off an eventful trip to the barn.

Fanny and Queen bolted and I took a nosedive through Queen's singletree. As they raced along I tried to haul in the

"*I*magine seeing our horse flipping toward the barn..."

lines as I slipped back onto the rake.

Familiar places on our farm whizzed past me as the rake swung wildly from side to side. After a few hundreds yards I went head over heels off the rake as it broke free from the hitch and did a cartwheel.

Fanny and Queen continued their mad race for the barn. When they reached the building they were going so fast they couldn't make the turn into the stable.

Horse Flipped into the Barn

Fanny tried to go through the door but Queen's neck yoke hit the barn. Imagine what it was like for a boy to see an animal the size of a horse flip through the air.

Queen ended up on her side with her feet sticking through the barn. Fortunately, even though we'd both taken a tumble, Queen and I weren't seriously injured.

My brother Paul grabbed her front legs, I grabbed the rear ones and we rolled Queen over. We put Queen and Fanny in their stalls for a little tender loving care.

For my mistake, they got a week off work. That's how long it took to repair the harness.

This happened back in the 1930's on our farm along Lake

Michigan's shores in Manitowoc County. Fanny and Queen replaced a couple of older horses on a farm owned by my father and operated by his youngest brother, Reuben.

Fanny and Queen were a team from the word "go". They also teamed up with my uncles for a few funny stories.

Uncle Needed New Clothes

Once Uncle Art needed a change of clothes and a pan of soapy water after working with Fanny and Queen. Art was using a fork to load manure into a spreader when the handle poked Queen in the ribs.

The lines were wrapped around the activator handle. When the team took off at a full gallop they began spreading manure everywhere except for where it was intended.

Uncle Art ran after the spreader. The team had run across a 20-acre field by the time Uncle Art climbed from the back to the front of the spreader to get the team stopped. What a mess that turned out to be for Uncle Art!

It's been over 50 years since the farm was sold, but my memories of Fanny and Queen are still as fresh as ever.

Betts Anderson/Unicorn Stock Photos

THE LAST LAUGH was often had by a clever horse or mule, according to many of their amused owners.

Chapter Five

Poignant Impressions

*D*ON'T BE SURPRISED if some of the following stories leave you with a lump in your throat.

We've already touched on the impact made by horses and mules on their owners and others who worked with them. In this chapter we delve a little more deeply into the relationship between people and their equine partners, a relationship which often took a bittersweet turn due to circumstances beyond human control.

As the age of four-legged horsepower gave way to the mechanization era, it was inevitable that some tough decisions would have to be made, often concerning whether to trade the team for a tractor. Still, farm and ranch folks didn't make these decisions lightly and probably not without a good deal of soul-searching as well.

Anyone who remembers a favorite team will surely appreciate the emotions described by these writers.

Bonnie Nance

Faithful Team Seemed to Sense What Owner Needed

By Mrs. Clifford Chandler, Loma, Montana

*A*FTER THE CHILDREN in our family grew up and left home, Dad did all the farm chores himself, including hauling hay to the cattle and horses.

During one visit, I looked out the window as Dad pulled up to the gate with the hayrack. The team stopped, and both horses looked around and watched as Dad slowly climbed down and opened the gate. His arthritic knees made this a painful task.

When Dad stood still, the team walked through the gate and stopped. The horses watched again as Dad slowly and painfully climbed onto the hayrack. Once he was seated and picked up the reins, the horses proceeded to the far end of the field, where they carefully crossed the ditch at a shallow spot.

"Mother," I said, "those horses watch Dad as if they know he has bad knees. Does he ever tell them when to stop?"

"No," she replied. "He never utters a word to them. They just seem to know what he wants them to do."

Dad had a good and faithful team, and I was very thankful for that.

They Sure Fooled Her

By Pat Halverson, Oneida, Wisconsin

I'VE ALWAYS loved horses. Even as a little girl living in the big city, I wanted a pony of my very own. So when we moved to a farm that had a team of workhorses, I was absolutely delighted.

I was 6 years old and did everything I could to make friends with "Dick" and "Cub". They were very patient and must have sensed how much I liked them, if not from my frequent brushing then from all the apples I fed them!

A year or two later, Dad decided I could start driving the wagon for haying. I was really proud when he told me I was doing a good job and "never missed a corner", meaning the loader could always pick up all the hay because I'd driven the team correctly around the corners.

A few years later, the team was sold. I was heartbroken—driving the tractor to help Dad with the haying just wasn't the same. I missed a lot of corners.

One day, after listening to Dad explain for the "umpteenth" time how to turn the corner correctly, I blurted out, "I never had this trouble with Dick and Cub! How come I always did okay with them?"

With a twinkle in his eye, Dad replied, "Those two ol' boys knew exactly what they were doing. When you told them to turn, they just ignored you if it was the wrong time.

"They'd been bringing in the hay for so long they really didn't need a driver. But you were enjoying yourself, and it was building your confidence, so I figured it was good for you."

I have never forgotten Dad's indulgence…or Dick and Cub's patience and understanding!

Blizzard Couldn't Thwart 'Bill's' Stamina

By Charles Dauk, Madison Lake, Minnesota

MY DAD purchased "Bill" and "Molly" in 1935 for $300. They were 5 and 6 years old, a Clydesdale-Hambletonian cross, and weighed about 1,500 pounds apiece. They were gentle but had lots of spirit. They never refused to pull or do anything we asked of them. We used them on all the farm machinery, besides hauling cream to town across the frozen lake in winter and also to get my brothers and sisters to school in bad weather.

In November 1940, I was engaged to be married. Two days before the wedding, our area was hit by the terrible Minnesota Armistice Day blizzard, which struck with 60-mile winds and dumped more than 20 inches of snow on us. Many lives were lost.

Because all roads were blocked for several days, the only way to reach my fiance, Lucille, was to ride Bill the 5 miles to her place. He got me there in fine shape, and we decided to postpone the wedding for 2 days.

My Dad gave us the team as a wedding present, and they continued to serve us faithfully for many more years. Lucille and I have been married 54 years, and I still get a lump in my throat when I remember Bill and Molly.

MEMORABLE GIFT. Charles and Lucille Dauk received this Clydesdale-Hambletonian team, "Bill" and "Molly", as a wedding present from Charles' father in 1940.

Memory of Childhood Ride Still Soothes Her Spirit

By Shirley Ostrander, Englewood, Florida

*T*HE FIRST TIME I fell in love was with our big gray Percherons. They were my constant companions. As a young girl growing up on a Pennsylvania farm, I spent hours with them in the barn on snowy and rainy days, telling them my hopes and dreams. They listened patiently, munching on the extra rations of oats I provided. When I was old enough, I loved to brush and curry them and help Dad and Grandpa clean their stalls.

One day when I was about 6, I decided to go for a ride. It was a Sunday afternoon, and Mom and Dad were taking a nap—no one would know! I bridled "Tom", opened the barn door, then climbed up the side of the stall and slid over onto his huge back. He never moved until I was safely seated. He seemed to know he had to take care of me. One word from me and we were out the door.

Our destination was the apple orchard, which was filled with the pink and white blossoms of spring. I still take that ride in my mind today, whenever I'm looking for peace and contentment. I'm never disappointed.

Schoolmarm Recalls Comfort-Seeking Horses

By Julia E. Espel, Princeton, Illinois

A FRIGHTENING RACE with an unruly partner left our little spotted horse, "Spot", shaken and badly in need of comfort.

The unsettling events began earlier during the day when Spot was teamed with a wild bronco we called "Montana".

Dad had been using Spot and Montana to mow hay. He decided they were too unreliable for that job. Dad exchanged them for the team I was using to cultivate corn.

I continued cultivating and all went well until Spot's lines came loose, something that occasionally happened. As I went to reattach them, Montana spooked, pulling Spot away with

> *"Spot trembled like a leaf, his head on my shoulder..."*

him in a race across the field.

By the time they'd reached the other side the cultivator and harness were broken. Montana ran off, leaving Spot behind. I began walking back to the house, figuring Dad could catch the horses later.

Walking down the lane, I heard a loud whinny behind me. There stood Spot with a woebegone look on his face.

Spot trembled like a leaf and held his head on my shoulder all the way home. It was obvious he was mighty upset by

Montana's shenanigans and needed reassurance—maybe he wanted to make certain he wasn't going to be blamed!

Unshod Mare Had Slippery Time

Another time I had to rescue an old mare I was driving to school during the first year I taught, 1928-29. The roads were so slippery with ice I had to find another way for her to walk home.

The 3-mile trip seemed a lot longer after a January ice storm. Unfortunately, the mare hadn't been shod and was slipping and falling repeatedly. After her third fall, I had to crawl over the ice on my hands and knees to get her unhitched.

I talked to the mare to keep her quiet and led her off the road. When we got into the grassy ditch, she could break through an icy crust and get some traction.

I left the buggy for Dad to fetch later. The mare and I followed the ditches home.

That weekend my brother led her into town to be shod. I don't know if her shoes were stylish, but I do know she appreciated being able to walk without falling the rest of that icy winter!

Fleeing Team Left Harness in Tatters

By R.G. McDonald, Thompsontown, Pennsylvania

WHEN I WAS 5, we moved to a farm in Millerstown, Pennsylvania and Dad bought a team of horses at a sheriff's sale. The lead horse, a big gray mare, was a retired cavalry horse—but she was afraid of snakes.

I was big for my age, and started plowing with the team when I was 8. One day the gray stepped on a black snake and spooked. Both horses bolted.

The plow flew up and got caught on a tree stump, the harness tore in pieces, and the horses just kept running. When Dad found them the next morning, all that was left of the harness was the collar and hames and one trace chain.

Our next team was a powerful pair of Belgian mares, "Maude" and "Doll". In spring, I'd drive them to the lime kiln every morning on the way to school and load 55 bushels of

"*The harness tore in pieces and the horses just kept running...*"

lime. They waited in the school yard, tied to an oak tree, until lunchtime. Then I brought them home, unloaded the lime and put them in the pasture. When Dad bought a threshing machine a few years later, they regularly pulled that up the hill behind the barn.

By the time I joined the service in 1944, Dad was no longer able to farm, and the horses had to be sold. When I came home from Germany, I farmed with a tractor—but it just wasn't the same. I'll never forget my team.

TREASURED TEAM. Ewald Ballweg of Roxbury, Wisconsin treasured this photo of his hardworking team, bought for $160 around 1937. "Queen", the horse at right, later was sold because she developed frequent colds. "Prince", at left, was sold much later, and Ewald's wife, Katie, was so heartbroken she cried for days. Their granddaughter, Diane Barfknecht of Baraboo, Wisconsin, shared this photo.

MULE MAN Andrew R. Bachman posed proudly with eight of his mules in the 1930's. "I can still remember Dad planting corn with his teams," writes Andrew's son, Tilman, of Roanoke, Illinois. "He'd plant a half-day with one team and would switch to another team after lunch. The mules' ears would go back and forth as the planter clicked. On a good day, Dad could plant 20 acres.

"I also remember when he purchased his first tractor. One day a big truck came and all of the mules were loaded on it, so I assume Dad traded them for the tractor. I'm sure he must have had tears in his eyes as the truck drove away, as he always loved his mules."

Stately Horses Left Lasting Impression

By Cornelia Highfell, Coos Bay, Oregon

HUGE TRACKS from horses even bigger than my childish imagination ignited a blazing curiosity in our Louisiana country grade school.

Just how big could these animals really be? That question had us children buzzing.

The Cajun ponies and Indian horses used on our farms around Lake Charles were small. They didn't leave tracks anywhere near as large as these new ones we'd found. Our curiosity continued to grow until one day teams of the larger animals were driven by our school.

We raced to the windows and pressed our faces against the glass. It was the first time we'd seen Belgian and Percheron horses.

It was as stunning as later in life when I saw my first airplane. These horses' hooves looked as large as dinner plates!

It was almost 80 years ago that the huge horses arrived in Louisiana with farmers from Missouri. The hardworking people were lured by an investment company's advertisement for better land at cheaper prices.

I had many more opportunities to see these spectacular horses. The newcomers liked to drive by our southern home.

The road was lined with cypress trees. Dad had planted corn and velvet beans along our lane, which intrigued our new neighbors from Missouri.

Unfortunately, their big horses weren't well suited for our sweltering summers. Eventually, most of the Missouri people moved back north.

We were no longer able to enjoy the sight of the majestic Belgian and Percheron horses. Thankfully, visions of them are stamped as deeply in my memory as their hoofprints were in our country road.

"THE BEST HORSES I ever trained were a pair of Percherons, half-brothers named 'Jim' and 'Buster'," says Harold Uhrmacher. The Superior, Nebraska farmer is now 80 and still remembers the team of black horses that worked in his fields and the neighbors' as well, mowing hay and cultivating potatoes. "They were tops!" Harold recalls.

TAKING A BREAK. Mr. and Mrs. John Gardner paused while working in their cornfield with horse "Bill" in North Lima, Ohio. Daughter Sophia Schmidt of New Middletown, Ohio says the photo was taken around 1924.

Horses Helped City Folks Learn to Farm

By Harold G. Neumann, Kalamazoo, Michigan

*A*S CITY SLICKERS new to a Michigan farm, our most interesting lessons were taught by our horses. Thanks to those five characters, the most memorable time of my life began in 1931. My parents, George and Laura Neumann, moved my sister and me from Chicago to a 200-acre farm in Van Buren County.

How exciting it was when we first became acquainted with our four-legged partners. Each had a unique personality which we needed to recognize for safety, efficiency and a few laughs, too.

"Ted" was the crew's senior citizen. Ted tired easily except when called to the barn.

I ran to chase him in. Ted only trotted to keep ahead of me. At times he tried to kick some spark into his step but his hooves barely came off the ground.

Ted's attempts at kicking were comical. On the other hand, "Nancy" kicked so hard and with such accuracy that we had to be extra cautious while working around her.

Nancy's value was as a tireless worker. She would still prance even after a long day in our fields.

Her partner, "Nellie", wasn't so spirited but was an uncomplaining, steady worker. Nellie had none of Nancy's unpredictable nature.

"Bessie", a heavy, short-coupled mare, flexed her thick muscles to work with little effort. Bessie was quiet and docile. She seldom fussed unless Dad bothered her at the horse trough.

Bessie Inherited Treasured Traits

Dad called Bessie "The Dowager Queen" because she'd inherited her ancestors' best traits. Bessie's intelligence showed when a soft voice or touch on a line could guide her through a quickly-mastered task.

"Prince" was a blaze-faced roan. He ruled the herd when Nancy wasn't around to show him who really was boss.

Prince was also an outlaw. Once after emptying a bag of popcorn, Prince tried to bite the hands that fed him.

Prince chased Mom and Sis under the low branches of a tree. I came by and caught him circling, waiting for them to

---

"Each horse had a unique personality we needed to know for safety and efficiency..."

---

come out. I distracted Prince while they ran for the house.

Afterwards we would chuckle about our horses teaching us new farmers about the dangers of hand-feeding a horse or sneaking up behind it.

Dad loved our horses and showed us how to work with their peculiarities. Dad never raised his voice or struck them for a mistake or quirky behavior.

Each evening we went with Dad to the barn and enjoyed the soothing music of horses crunching grain and hay while resting in their stalls.

Dad patted their necks and fed them treats of sugar bran or sliced apple. Dad said the treats were to reinforce his appreciation for helping us earn our new living.

Many of the country lessons Sis and I learned from our loving parents and our horses have helped guide us throughout our lives.

Brother Treated Injured Horse

By Lillian DiVincent, North Bergen, New Jersey

*T*HE SIGHT OF AN INJURED HORSE once made my brother part with money we needed for important family necessities.

Mike came home from the fair with two horses instead of the money. At first, Mother was so mad she cried. As it turned out, our family ended up loving those horses.

This all started back in the 1930's when Mike went to the county fairgrounds in West Virginia. We raised most of our own food but got money for necessities with the occasional sale of a calf or pig.

Mike was walking home after making such a sale and saw two horses in a pasture. One had deep barbed wire cuts and looked like it didn't have long to live.

Mike complained to the farmer but must not have liked his response. Mike ended up buying both the horses.

Responded to Kindness

The horses had become ill-tempered due to their neglect. Each day my brother talked nicely to them, healing their injured personalities while he doctored the one horse's cuts.

We named them "Babe" and "Molly". Through the tireless attention from my brother, Babe and Molly became a working team …and our favorite animals on the farm.

"BABE" AND "MOLLY" became family favorites after kind attention from Lillian DiVincent's brother, Mike.

I loved them so much that it was very hard when we had to part with them and move to New Jersey. To this day, I'm convinced those horses appreciated my brother's efforts on their behalf and repaid his kindness with their hard work and lasting affection.

Frightened Team Raced To Early Retirement

By Mary S. Beer, Hamilton, Montana

A SPLIT DECISION by our team of horses ruined a wagon and ended their careers in our hay fields.

After the horses' mishap I guess my husband thought it was time to retire old "Tony" and "Dick" and try a tractor.

It all began on a summer morning back in the 1950's. My husband and 9-year-old son were putting up hay, and our son let his hayfork get caught up in the chopper.

The terrible racket startled Tony and Dick, the team that was hauling the hay. The team bolted down the lane toward the house, with the wagon rattling and banging along behind.

I heard the commotion and looked out the window in time to see them racing by. My hopes that they wouldn't get out on the paved road were fulfilled, but not exactly in the way I'd wanted.

As they approached an open gate, Tony kept heading for the lane. Dick decided to run through the opening and into an alfalfa field.

Horses Stopped in Their Tracks

The horses hit the gate post. The crash stopped them right in their tracks. They were lucky to have escaped any serious injury.

The harness and wagon weren't as lucky. They were damaged beyond repair.

Dick was a placid horse but Tony skittish. After that incident, my husband decided to eliminate the possibility of any animal error during our haying operation.

He went out and bought a used John Deere tractor. It performed faithfully for many years, but my husband always claimed it wasn't the same as farming with horses. I was never entirely sure whether he meant that in a positive or negative sense—a little of both, I suspect!

"OUR PARENTS, Andrew and Sara Streit, owned 22 horses in the 1920's and '30's and used them extensively for farming and transportation on our place in northeast Kansas," writes Clyde Streit of Kerrville, Texas. "We often rode ponies to school, as in the picture of me seated behind my brother Wesley with our older brother Leonard standing next to us.

"My folks resisted buying a tractor for a long time. Dogs are said to be man's best friend, but we considered our horses to be our best friends because of their hard work. Our whole family, including my older brother Reuben (below), always enjoyed working with horses!"

Percherons Pulled Farmer's Hearse

By Beth Keese, Gilman, Iowa

FOND MEMORIES of Percherons from my husband's childhood remained with him all his life.

In fact, my husband, Larry, loved the horses so much that two black Percherons pulled the hearse at his funeral.

Larry's love for Percherons started with stories from his father, who owned a team of black Percherons named "Buster" and "Byrd". One cold day during the 1940's Larry's father used the team to rescue a man's truck from a ditch.

Larry's father had hired the man to spread lime on their back field. The trucker tried to drive across a creek that appeared frozen and buried his vehicle up to its axle.

He trudged to the house to call for a tow. The truck was loaded with 4 tons of lime.

Larry's father volunteered to put the Percherons to work. He rounded up Buster and Byrd, harnessed them and headed for the creek.

The horses were so eager to pull that Larry's father had to hurry to get their chain hooked to the truck. In just an instant the heavily-loaded vehicle was on dry ground.

This was one of Larry's favorite stories. I lost my husband when he was killed in a tractor accident in October of 1994.

Out of respect for Larry's love for horses, we had a team of black Percherons pull his hearse to Graceland Cemetery just west of Laurel, Iowa.

'Ted' Kept Farm Girl Remembering

By Avis Sergeant Warner, Lemmon, South Dakota

FAITHFUL "TED" taught me how well horses can remember things.

As a girl growing up in South Dakota, I never missed an opportunity to drive Ted. And that smart horse never missed a chance to turn into the lane leading to the farm where he was born.

Most times I was able to haul back on the lines hard enough so Ted couldn't turn. Ted would try this almost every time we were on the main road and passed that familiar lane.

Ted was born in 1913, the same year I was born. I didn't

> ## "*Old Ted never missed the turn to the farm where he was born...*"

realize that until I was about 5 years old and Dad was breaking Ted to drive.

As a young gelding, Ted was a beautiful, gleaming black. Later he turned to dapple gray and Dad bought a mare the same color to hitch with Ted. What a beautifully matched pair they were.

Dad would let me drive them to water after he came in from the field. By the time I was 8 years old, I was driving them on the hayrack, freeing Dad to pitch hay.

Drove Ted to Town

Later I learned to drive the buggy and was allowed to take Ted to town, about 3 miles away. Even with my eyes closed I could always tell when we were approaching the farm where Ted was born.

Ted would trot faster, hoping that speed would prevent me from stopping his attempt to turn down that lane.

Ted worked when I wasn't taking him off to town. We used him to cultivate corn and vegetables. Ted worked for us long after Dad passed away.

Ted was with us until we had to sell the farm and him with it. Ted lived to be 30 and we would visit him from time to time at the old place. I always wondered if he continued to try to turn down that lane whenever he was driven to town!

"TED" was born same year as Avis Warner, later became dapple gray.

Faithful Pair Teamed Forever

By Ruthann Johns, Woodburn, Indiana

NOTHING COULD SEPARATE our most faithful team of horses, "Bud" and "Dais".

One dark spring night we looked in our field and found that Bud and Dais were gone. We'd hoped that they were together, so we could avoid doubling our efforts to find them. Dad also feared an accident on the road or railroad tracks.

But he found Bud and Dais calmly grazing together in another farmer's field. Dad came to get me because I was skilled at coaxing them along with treats.

I led Bud back home. As always, Dais was following faithfully alongside.

What a team they were. Bud was as white as Dais was black. Dais had a bright star glittering in one eye.

Dad raised Bud from a colt. After Dad trained Bud, he bought Dais from an Amish farmer.

Team Loved Working Together

Right from the beginning, Bud and Dais worked well when hitched as a team. Bud was the leader and Dais would follow eagerly.

After their first few steps each morning, Dad didn't even have to hold the lines. Bud and Dais were always a step ahead in getting the job done.

My pleasant job was to take treats to Bud and Dais each morning. Then the kind, affectionate horses would follow me back to the barn for work.

When Bud and Dais became too old to work, Dad retired them to pasture. No way would he have gotten rid of Bud and Dais.

Old Bud spent his last day with me holding his head in my arms. On Bud's departure, Dais either lost her spirit or was still intent on following her partner's lead.

She left us a month later. Bud and Dais now rest together on the farm where they so enjoyed their life as a team.

Mother Bathed 'Bird' and 'Betsy'

By G. H. Price, Portland, Ohio

MOTHER'S TENDER CARE of our workhorses tops my memories of farm life in Ohio decades ago.

How she fretted after "Bird" and "Betsy" when they would come in from a hard day pulling in our fields. I can still see the team trotting up to the barn.

Bird and Betsy plunged their noses deep into the water trough. We would take the bits out of their mouths to make it easier for them to drink.

Usually the horses were covered with lather. Mother would bring a sponge and soapy water to bathe the horses' shoulders.

Those horses worked hard in hot weather, but Mother sure looked after them. She made sure they stayed fit and healthy.

We loved all our horses and mules, even though some of them weren't as dependable as Bird and Betsy.

"Harry" was a balker. Sometimes Harry would work steadily, but other times he'd stop working and lie down. And he would stay down until he was good and ready to get up!

Sometimes that might be 5 minutes. But occasionally it was 5 hours, and that sure took a bite out of the workday.

Still, life on the farm back in the 1920's through the 1940's was a wonderful existence for a boy, and our horses and mules contributed a lot to that.

Horses Took Tractor's Place

By Louise Allen, Mason, Michigan

BELGIAN AND PERCHERON horses replaced our tractor when we grew tired of working with machinery.

My late husband, Harry, was in his early 50's when we decided to turn back time and work with horses. Harry said he'd always had horses in his blood and needed them around again.

Harry's father, Martin, drove teams of horses when they

were building the roads in our rural Michigan area. Harry's grandfather was a Civil War cavalry veteran.

Harry was using nine horses on his dairy farm near Lansing when we met in 1933. We married in 1935 and raised four children on what we earned from farming with horses.

Eventually, we turned to tractors as the farming business became more demanding. But in 1968, we began using horses again.

It took longer to hitch horses than it did to start a tractor. But we never had to call an expensive mechanic to repair a horse, Harry was fond of saying.

Working with horses was so interesting that Harry always was able to hire boys to help. I used to drive a team when we put up hay.

In 1970 we moved farther north in Michigan and began giving sleigh rides in the wintertime. Over the years we had a total of 65 Belgian and Percheron horses. Our favorites were the dapple grays.

We were quite proud of the team of dapple-gray Percherons that we sold to the Hanneford Circus in Florida. An even greater honor was bestowed on another pair of dapple-gray Percherons.

When Harry passed away in 1986, those beautiful Percherons pulled the hearse that carried Harry to his final resting place.

Harry had requested his last ride not be in anything powered by an engine.

FOND FAREWELL. Louise Allen honored husband Harry's wish to have Percherons take him to his final resting place.

Terry Koper

Chapter Six

Carrying on the Tradition

*A*LTHOUGH most of the preceding stories have been about favorite teams remembered from earlier times, there are plenty of folks still using draft horses and mules in their farming operations today.

For some, it's a way of remaining in touch with a simpler, more fulfilling way of life. For others, it may be a hobby based on a deep-rooted love of the animals themselves.

Whatever their reasons, these people share a common belief that there's nothing quite as satisfying as following a good team through the fields. They just plain like working with horses or mules, and—as several contributors stated—they can't imagine not doing so.

We saved this selection of stories and photos for the last chapter as a tribute to those who are keeping the tradition alive for future generations. One person wrote, "As long as there's farming, there will always be a place for horses and mules." We couldn't agree more.

THESE HIGH-STEPPING MULES, owned by Bill and Janice Mytton (above) of Arena, Wisconsin, are used for a variety of purposes. Besides farming with the team, the Myttons enjoy exhibiting them at mule and draft horse shows and driving them in parades and historical re-enactments. At left, Bill removes the harness from one of his long-eared friends after a day's work.

Logger Would Rather Work Mules than Eat!

By Peggy Young, Irvine, Kentucky

MY HUSBAND uses a pair of mules, "Zeb" and "Zeke", for logging on our farm. James has worked with mules all his life. Even when he's hungry, he'd rather work with mules than eat.

Zeb and Zeke do pretty much what James tells them. He has them broken to the point where he lets them go on their own with a log, using voice commands to make them stop or turn.

James prefers mules to mechanized equipment because he says they don't tear up as much wood as 'dozers and skidders do. They don't cost as much, either. In one day, James can pull out $3,000 worth of logs at a cost of about $100.

What's more, Zeb and Zeke are gentle, strong and graceful creatures. You can't say that about a bulldozer!

"Mules don't play or fool around," James says. "They work for a living—theirs, and mine, too!"

SKIDDING LOGS. James Young uses his mule team, "Zeb" and "Zeke", to skid logs on his Kentucky farm. Wife Peggy says the mules are more economical and cause less damage to the logs than mechanized equipment. Son Matthew was just shy of his first birthday when he was photographed aboard Zeb. Dad James says he hopes Matthew will also grow up to be a muleskinner. Looks like he's off to a good start!

Horses Add Quality to Iowa Lifestyle

By E. Johlas, Charles City, Iowa

JUST THE OTHER DAY we were reminded again of the important role horses still play in Iowa life.

It was such a pleasant sight to see our friend and neighbor, Don Ritter, training young workhorses. Don and his son, Doug, were working with a pair of beautiful paint horses.

Don has lived and worked with horses all his life. His mother said he learned to ride a horse before he could walk.

Their family still works with horses, raises them and drives their teams in parades. Don has driven teams in parades all around our part of Iowa.

Don is most proud of driving a team in the Milwaukee Circus Parade. Another of his outstanding accomplishments occurred back in 1961, though it is of a different nature.

After a blizzard closed roads that year, Don hitched his horses to a bobsled. He drove the team to the general store in Powersville and shuttled supplies to stranded farmers.

Don still hauls manure, mows hay and gives plowing demonstrations with a team of Percherons named "Dick" and "Duke".

Don and his wife, LaVonne, have been farming with horses for 45 years at their place near Greene, Iowa. We're proud to have such fine neighbors and to see someone continuing this tradition!

Farmer Turns Back Clock With Modern Teams

By Clarence Nordstrom, Pine City, Minnesota

I GREW UP in Minnesota working with horses. After I got married in 1938 and started farming on my own, we continued using horses.

Even though I'm now 79, I still enjoy working with horses, as do many other rural people.

I started competing in plowing contests back in 1965. I

believe these contests have done a lot to revive the interest in workhorses.

I compete in the walking plow class. I also drive nine horses on a three-bottom gang plow. That always attracts a lot of attention. It reminds me of my younger days, when we used "Ned" in our nine-horse hitch.

Ned was born in 1961 and lived more than 25 years. He was a handsome chestnut gelding with a light mane and tail and a white blaze on his face.

He weighed over 2,100 pounds and could out-pull any other animal we ever owned. To this day people still recall Ted and ask about him when we have teams in parades and at the county fair. I have taken horses to the county fair since I was 14.

Back in those days I'd hurry home from school so I wouldn't miss my Dad plowing. I'd walk with him and sometimes Dad would let me hold the plow. A few times he even let me hold the lines.

I still get excited every time I pick up a set of lines. I intend to keep at least one team of horses as long as I live!

LONG-TIME HORSEMAN
Clarence Nordstrom of Pine City, Minnesota says people still ask about "Ned" (below), one of the best horses Clarence ever owned. Clarence now competes in walking plow competitions with mother-son team "Lady" and "Prince" (right) and also drives a six-horse hitch on a John Deere two-bottom plow (below right).

Team Takes Kids Back to Good Old Days

By LaMar J. Ashby, Smithfield, Utah

FARMING WITH HORSES is a lot easier today than it was back in my father's time.

That's because I always have a lot more volunteer help than Dad did. All I have to do is start to hitch up a team and my friends and their kids come running.

In my younger days we weren't so eager to chase after work when Dad went for the team. Still, I loved working with our horses.

We farmed in Utah with a team of horses and an old home-made tractor. I drove that team a lot.

When I got older I had to take a town job. All my adult life I still wanted to buy a team, even if it was just for the fun of being around horses again.

It probably wouldn't be hard for anybody to guess my first major purchase when I retired. You're right if you guessed horses.

Just over 3 years ago, I finally bought my very own team. What a pair they are!

"Nettie" is a Clydesdale and "Pal" is a Percheron, and they weigh about 1,700 pounds apiece. They're as gentle as puppies and a real pleasure to work and drive.

The biggest decision I ever have to make now is choosing which helper will drive first. Then all I have to do is tell them what needs doin' and it gets done.

Drive for Fun

We drive Nettie and Pal to plow and to make hay. Their most important job, however, is letting people have fun while getting a little taste of what life was like when most of the country was powered by horses or mules.

When it comes to working, Nettie and Pal are just an average team, I guess. Like a lot of older, well-trained horses, they start and stop when they are told. Most times the lines aren't even needed to drive them.

They are very affectionate also. When I see them with my

children and grand-
children, I know that
horses will always play
an important part in
people's lives.

QUITE AN ATTRACTION!
*LaMar Ashby of Smithfield,
Utah says harnessing up
"Nettie" and "Pal" is all he has
to do to bring people running, eager to help out with
the horses.*

**FATHER-AND-
SON TEAM.**
"The Harlow
Post family of St.
Albans, Maine
uses draft horse
teams year
'round on their
farm," writes
Ruth Fluet of
Skowhegan,
Maine. "Father
and son have
over 50 years'
combined expe-
rience working
with horses."

GIDDAP! Donna Thompson fulfills a lifelong dream, driving a team of draft horses, on her farm near Dousman, Wisconsin. The horses are owned by Tom Maule (shown above with Donna and checking planter box, below), a member of the Jefferson County Draft Horse Association. Tom dropped by to plant an oats and pasture mix on Donna's acres and wound up giving her a driving lesson as well.

MEMBERS of the Jefferson County Draft Horse Association frequently get together to stage field day demonstrations in their home state of Wisconsin. Many of the members also use their horses for farming on their own acres.

Skinner Plans to Drive Team Into 21st Century

By John B. Hogoboom, El Dorado, Kansas

*I*F I'M STILL EARNING my keep in the next century, it'll be due to the lessons I learned from horses starting over 80 years ago.

I began working with horses in Kansas about the same time I started grade school. I'm in my mid-80's now and still don't need any help to harness or hitch up my teams.

When I was 7 years old, I started working with a team and a wagon, taking odd jobs around town. Some days I'd only make a few cents and on others I'd make up to 3 dollars, which was mighty big money back then.

Today I still drive teams, and now I'm a wagon master. Over 20 years ago, I helped start a wagon train for folks who want to sample pioneer life and be around horses. Every year the wagon train has become more popular.

People from all over the country come to Kansas to take part in our wagon train. Throughout the summer we have six covered wagons taking people on 2-day trips across the Kansas prairie to the Flint Hills.

They see life as it was when I was a tyke looking out of the back of a wagon. I rode in a covered wagon with my parents as they searched for a place to settle and homestead.

I farmed with mules as a youngster, and in the 1920's I got a job working mules in an oil field. I used them to haul heavy equipment.

When World War II broke out, I was driving a team of horses to build grades for the railroad. Then a pipeline company hired me to plow a fire guard around its large oil barrels to prevent sabotage.

I learned a lot working with horses and mules, and I even wrote a book back in 1965 about my experiences. No matter how the country changes, there will always be a place for these great animals.

I have also changed with the times, but I still own six horses and continue to make my living with them. I'll be a "long-line skinner" until my last sundown!